Insights and Inspirations from Reggio Emilia

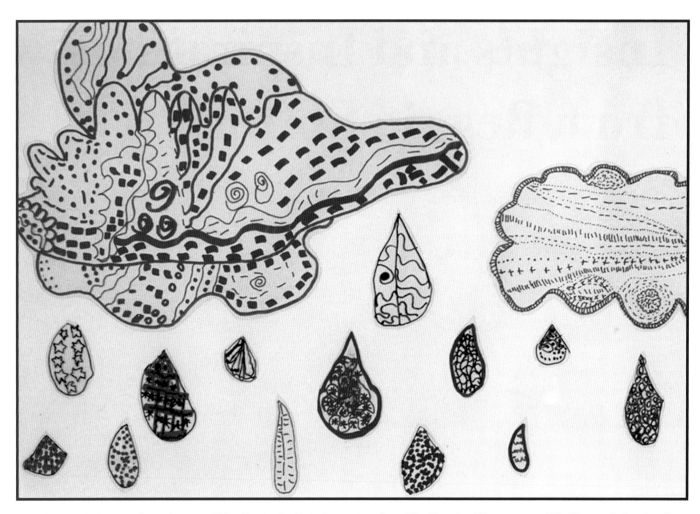

The children's design of raindrops in "The City in the Rain," a project from The Hundred Languages of Children exhibit that first traveled the United States in 1987.

Insights and Inspirations from Reggio Emilia

Stories of Teachers and Children from North America

Edited by Lella Gandini, Susan Etheredge, and Lynn Hill

Davis Publications, Inc. Worcester, Massachusetts

Photographs from Reggio Children are reproduced by permission.
The photographs below are reproduced by permission by Reggio Children s.r.l. Via Bligny 1/A 42100
Reggio Emilia Italy, (e-mail **info@reggiochildren.it**, website **www.reggiochildren.it**)
The copyright © is Preschools and Infant-toddler Centers—Istituzione of the Municipality of Reggio Emilia and Reggio Children, Italy

p. 21	Drawing the project "The City and the Rain" from the Catalog of the Exhibit "The Hundred Languages of Children", published by Reggio Children
p. 33	Portrait Loris Malaguzzi for the Lego Prize.
p. 37	Malaguzzi & Hawkins at La Villetta Preschool.
p. 39	Teachers & 5 year olds, Anna Frank Preschool (dinosaur project).
p. 91	Cover publication "Noi Bimbi e lui Gulliver", Ada Gobetti Preschool.
p. 93	Drawing from the above publication.
pp. 136–137	Three dimensional bicycles by children at REMIDA Recycling Center
p.149	Drawing from the project "The City and the rain" from the Catalog of the Exhibit "The Hundred Languages of Children", published by Reggio Children
p.173	Group Photograph. Seminar June 1994, Reggio Emilia
pp.139–141	Some of the images on these pages are reprinted with permission of the Publisher. From Lella Gandini, Lynn Hill, Louise Cadwell, and Charles Schwall, *In the Spirit of the Studio: Learning from the Atelier of Reggio Emilia*, New York: Teachers College Press, © 2005 by Teachers College, Columbia University. All rights reserved.

Copyrighted material by Mary Hartzell and Joanne Mandakas reproduced by permission.

A portion of the royalties from this publication will go to Reggio Children: International Center for the Defense and Promotion of the Rights and Potential of All Children.

ISBN: 978-0-87192-894-8

13 12 11 10 09 08   10 9 8 7 6 5 4 3 2 1

Publisher: Wyatt Wade
Managing Editor: David Coen
Production & Manufacturing Manager: Georgiana Rock
Editorial Assistance: Missy Nicholson, Annette Cinelli, Reba Libby
Design: Greta Merrick, Douglass Scott, WGBH DESIGN

Printed in China

To our colleagues in Reggio Emilia
who continue the work of Loris Malaguzzi,
creating connections with and among cultures and countries,
contributing ideas and strategies
for the well-being of all children, their teachers, and their parents.

"Learning is the key factor in which a new way of teaching
should be based, becoming a complementary resource
to the child and offering multiple options, suggestive ideas,
and sources of support.

Learning and teaching should not stand on opposite banks
and just watch the water flow by; instead,
they should embark together on a journey down the river.

Through an active, reciprocal exchange,
teaching can strengthen learning how to learn."

LORIS MALAGUZZI

History, Ideas, and Philosophy,
an interview with Lella Gandini in
The Hundred Languages of Children,
The Reggio Emilia Approach—Advanced
Reflections, 1998, Ablex Publications,
Westport, CT pp.83

Contents

Introductions

Section One
Loris Malaguzzi, Founder and Philosopher: His Image of the Child

Section Two
A Renewed Image of the Teacher

Section Three
Children, Thought, and Learning
Made Visible through Documentation

Section Four
The Hundred Languages of Children:
The Role of Materials and the Atelier

Section Five
The Power of Communication

Section Six
History and Civic Awareness:
Building Environments and Communities

Foreword Lessons from Reggio

Steve Seidel

Through a decade of collaboration and association around the Making Learning Visible project and through the friendships that have evolved in that time, we at Project Zero* have learned many lessons. These lessons have influenced virtually every aspect of our ways of being in the world, but certainly our understanding of schools, our teaching, our ways of working in collaborations, even how we are with family and friends.

The need for accountability in American education has been the cornerstone for the standards-driven reform movement of the 1990s and continues to dominate our educational thought and practice. We are, in this moment in the United States, so deeply invested in the idea of psychometric and "scientific" justifications for our educational practices that we seem to have forgotten there could be any other justification paradigm. We seem to have forgotten there could be any other way to hold ourselves accountable.

Some days I wonder if the path we're on is leading somewhere, or nowhere…is just difficult and long, or truly impossible. I would probably be far more confused—and despondent—if the Reggio experience didn't remind me of another possibility.

Reggio educators accept responsibility for their decisions and choices, for providing an account of what they are doing, and why, and what then happens in the school. They don't pass the assessment of their choices on to someone else or to a test to determine. They embrace a tradition of philosophical justification that is far older than psychometrics, one that explains educational choices by tracing decisions back to basic questions about our image of the child, the teacher, the school.

In this psychometric age, philosophic justifications of educational practice are generally characterized as soft, vague, or lacking in rigor. Yet anyone who visits the schools in Reggio quickly recognizes there is no lack of rigor in what they do. Indeed, there is virtually no aspect of the classroom or school environment too small for deep and rigorous examination. Every moment of the day, every detail of the physical environment, every dimension of

*Project Zero, a research group at the Harvard Graduate School of Education, has investigated the development of learning processes in children, adults, and organizations since 1967.

relationships in the school is considered, debated, refined. Choices are examined in relation to the ideas that animate them and the actual experiences of children and teachers in the classroom. This is endless work. What is decided today is reconsidered next year, next week, or the next day.

Ironically, as attractive and inspiring as the Reggio schools are to so many American educators, most of us believe we don't have the time to think through our practice as they do. I don't think it is a problem of time so much as commitment to the deep level of rigorous thought and debate that infuses daily life in the Reggio schools. Perhaps we hesitate as we approach this alternative paradigm of accountability because we know instinctively that it is a difficult path, demanding much of those who follow it.

Yet it seems always better to be on a difficult—even extremely difficult—path than a path that, in my heart, I believe won't lead where I want to go. The challenge and beauty of coming to know the experience in Reggio is to confront the possibility that I could work—as they have—with others to create the reality I would like to live in…whatever the demands of that creative act.

Preface

The Editors

One great good fortune for young children, their parents, and their teachers has been the journey of ideas and practices developed in Reggio Emilia, Italy, into the North American educational context. A subsequent benefit has been the effort of thoughtful educators over time to interpret and reinvent those ideas and practices. They have done this in their infant/toddler centers and preschools or in teacher preparation programs, in harmony with their respective local communities and cultural contexts.

Here in this book is a varied and energizing sample of those interpretations, conducted in different places and from different perspectives. They all reflect a deep appreciation of the basic values of the Reggio Emilia philosophy, values that resonate with the historical roots of progressive education.

But why this book now?

We, as editors and contributors, want to offer to our colleagues in Reggio Emilia these expressions of gratitude for what they have offered and continue to offer us. We find the same intention and desire among all the contributors who joined in. The intent is to try to give, in return, visible and tangible evidence that documents today what began many years ago, even before the launching of The Hundred Languages of Children exhibit in California in 1987.[1]

Insights and Inspirations from Reggio Emilia captures and celebrates thirty years of the Reggio Emilia innovative presence and inspiration in North American early childhood educational thought and practice. It is a narrative in word and image, representing the voices of teachers, scholars, and policy makers whose professional philosophies and practices have been changed and, in many cases, truly transformed by their study of the Reggio Emilia approach. Each contribution tells a story (in narrative or poetic and visual form) that recounts experiences, lessons learned, reflections, reinterpretations, and initiatives connected with encounters with the philosophy and practices of Reggio. These signs of gratitude honor first and foremost the legacy of Loris Malaguzzi (1920–1994), who developed and constructed with collaborators and teachers what is now known around the world as the Reggio Emilia approach. These signs honor as well his colleagues who are continuing to develop his philosophy, using novel avenues fully in harmony with his dynamic original view of exploring new ways and new sources of learning that can create a diversity of connections and relationships.

The exhibition[1], a tribute to the many ways children have to communicate, first landed in the United States in 1987. Updated and revised in 1995, the exhibit describes and illustrates the philosophy and pedagogy of the Reggio Emilia approach through photographs that depict moments of teaching and learning, children's words, and samples of children's work such as paintings, collages, clay, and constructions. This beautiful and intriguing visual display narrates an educational story, weaving together experiences, reflections, debates, theoretical premises, and the social and ethical ideals of many generations of teachers, children, and parents.

We have invited contributions from those involved in the study of Reggio Emilia from its first presence in North America to those discovering and exploring the approach more recently. These include the voices of well-known and regarded scholars and administrators, as well as the active, perhaps less known, voices of the teachers in the everyday classroom, who give powerful witness to the effectiveness of the approach. The diversity of messages and stories gives value to the power of what has been learned from the encounter with the educators and schools of Reggio Emilia and of how it has been translated and reinvented, all the while respecting the experience and context of each person and place. To bring changes in one's own way of teaching requires a strong personal and political choice. Furthermore, to bring change in a school requires a social and democratic commitment by all involved, with the determination to build stronger relationships and collaborations.

As we worked to prepare this surprise for our friends in Reggio, we came to realize that it would not be possible to represent all of the dedicated and serious educators engaged in the transformation inspired by Reggio now taking place in North American preschools, public schools, child care centers, and infant/toddler centers. Thus, the most evident shortcoming of this book is that it contains only a limited number of voices.

Each contributor has submitted an image or images (photographs, a piece of children's work) to accompany her or his narrative. The images expand and enhance the written text and, conversely, the written text expands and enhances the images. The contributions reflect documentation and presentation in expressive languages—verbal as well as visual—in keeping with the spirit of the Reggio Emilia approach, which regards children as possessing a hundred different languages for learning and communicating—when adults provide them with the possibility.

Insights and Inspirations

This collection begins with a series of introductions that include a visual sign of gratitude from educator and author Cathy Weisman Topal ("Is It Possible to Say 'Thank You' with an Image?"); brief introductions to the schools and city of Reggio Emilia, including descriptions of the common values and principles that guide the ideas and pedagogy of the educators in that city, from educator and author Lella Gandini; and cognitive psychologist and author Jerome Bruner's homage to Reggio Emilia "from an honorary citizen." Here we learn why Professor Bruner returns every year to visit the city and the schools for young children where he found a way of learning and teaching close to the ideas he has worked for in education in the United States.

This book's six main sections are organized around major themes that emerged from the contributors' efforts. The first theme engages Loris Malaguzzi and what he termed "the image of the child" as currently presented in The Hundred Languages of Learning, the historic exhibit about early childhood education in Reggio Emilia. Malaguzzi was founder[2] of the public system of preschools and infant/toddler centers in Reggio Emilia, Italy. A tirelessly innovative and influential thinker, Malaguzzi placed great value on practice, both for the transformation of theory and, in turn, the generation of new ideas.

The Notes section at the end of the book provides interested readers with sources for quotations and further reading about these ideas.

The subsequent sections of the book are organized around these themes:

a renewed image of the teacher

children, thought, and learning made visible through documentation

the hundred languages of children: the role of materials and the atelier

the power of communication

history and civic awareness: building environments and communities

Each themed section begins with a brief overview of the contributions for that section and how each piece can serve for further reflection and inspire strategies for practice with children. We then introduce the section with commentary or reflection by Loris Malaguzzi, by his colleagues, and other educational leaders on the philosophy and practices of the Reggio Emilia approach. In our effort to engage not only teachers and preservice teachers but also those who themselves prepare these individuals, we the editors believe that these introductory passages hold much potential for further reflection and analysis.

We would like to thank many people who have helped us prepare this book, among them James McGuire, and, above all, Wyatt Wade of Davis Publications and his talented group of editors and designers.

We strongly hope that this book will serve as a useful source of information for those new to the Reggio Emilia approach and of support both for teachers who are beginning to explore the ideas of Reggio Emilia and for those who are working to refine their understanding of the approach.

Introductions

What does it mean to be inspired by Reggio?

"Reggio is a metaphor and a symbolic place.
Being in relation with Reggio allows people to hope,
to believe change is possible.
It enables you to cultivate dreams,
rather than being in a utopia.
Because a utopia is something very good but perfect;
instead dreams are something that you can have one night.
And there is also a feeling of belonging to something
that is about education in its widest sense,
as a hope for human beings.
And Reggio is a place of encounter and dialogue
and not only with Reggio but with many related protagonists.
So Reggio makes room for people to dialogue,
it provides an excuse to do this."

CARLINA RINALDI [1]

Is It Possible to Say "Thank You" with an Image?

Cathy Weisman Topal

A toddler walks out of our center with his father.
Puddles from a winter warm spell lie in wait.
Kyle walks directly into the biggest puddle and stops, transfixed.
He looks for a long time—long enough for me
to capture this moment with my camera.
Kyle's father looks on, intrigued,
understanding Kyle's need for time.
What is Kyle thinking? What is he noticing?
What are his questions?
A seemingly ordinary moment fraught with potential
can disappear so easily.
But the gifts that have come from Reggio
have changed the way I see children,
and the way in which I live in the world.

Introduction to the Schools of Reggio Emilia

Lella Gandini

Young children, their care, and their education have long been a public concern at various levels of Italian society. What families have obtained was not easy to achieve; it came from a great deal of effort and political involvement. Workers, educators, and especially women were active and effective advocates of the legislation that established public preschools in 1968 and infant/toddler centers in 1971. The results of the effort by all these determined people are publicly funded municipal as well as national programs for young children that combine the concept of social services with education. Both education and care are considered necessary to provide high quality, full-day experiences for young children.

In Italy now, preschools, whether municipal, national or private, serve about 95 percent of the children between the ages of three and six. Although the quantity of infant/toddler programs has been lower, the quality of these services in those municipalities that have invested seriously in them has been generally outstanding.

What, then, is so special about Reggio Emilia, a city of 140,000 inhabitants in northern Italy?

First of all, the city-run educational system for young children originated there in schools started by parents; literally groups of parents built them with their own hands at the end of World War II. The first school was built with proceeds from the sale of a tank, some trucks, and a few horses left behind by the retreating German army. Such participation by parents has all along remained an essential part of the way of working on education in that city.

Secondly, right from the start Loris Malaguzzi, then a young teacher, guided and directed the energies of those parents, later preparing teachers and becoming an educational leader not just in his hometown but also on the national scene.

Third, the tradition of cooperative work is firmly rooted in the Emilia Romagna region and is based on a sense of community and of solidarity. Through a strong sense of solidarity, people there are accustomed to construct and maintain the connections with the community. They typically respond to immediate, usually material needs, by forming cooperatives. Yet the spirit of cooperation that they engendered in such endeavors tends to transcend those needs to leave enduring marks upon the culture of their region.

Values and Principles of the Reggio Emilia

What are the distinguishing features of the education of young children with regard to theory and practice that have made the Reggio Emilia approach so notable?

An examination of the features of this philosophy soon reveals that the educators have been serious readers of John Dewey, Jean Piaget, Lev Vygotsky, David Hawkins, Jerome Bruner, Howard Gardner, and other world-renowned scientists and philosophers. In fact, Reggio Emilia educators have continued to keep abreast of the latest research in child development and education in other countries. At the same time, though, they continue to formulate new interpretations and new hypotheses and ideas about learning and teaching through their daily observations and practice of learning along with the children.

The image of the child. All children have preparedness, potential, curiosity; they have interest in relationship, in constructing their own learning, and in negotiating with everything the environment brings to them. Children should be considered as active citizens with rights, as contributing members, with their families, of their local community. Children with special rights (rather than using the term special needs) have precedence in becoming part of an infant/toddler center or a preschool.

Children's relationships and interactions within a system. Education has to focus on each child, not considered in isolation, but seen in relation with the family, with other children, with the teachers, with the environment of the school, with the community, and with the wider society. Each school is viewed as a system in which all these relationships, which are all interconnected and reciprocal, are activated and supported.

The role of parents. Parents are an essential component of the program—a competent and active part of their children's learning experience. They are not considered consumers but co-responsible partners. Their right to participation is expected and supported; it takes many forms and can help ensure the welfare of all children in the program.

The role of space: amiable schools. The infant/toddler centers and preschools convey many messages, of which the most immediate is: this is a place where adults have thought about the quality and the instructive power of space. The layout of physical space fosters encounters, communication, and relationships. Children learn a great deal in exchanges and negotiations with their peers; therefore teachers organize spaces that support the engagement of small groups.

Teachers and children as partners in learning. A strong image of the child has to correspond to a strong image of the teacher. Teachers are not considered protective babysitters, teaching basic skills to children but, rather, they are seen as learners along with the children. They are supported, valued for their experience and their ideas, and seen as researchers. Cooperation at all levels in the schools is the powerful mode of working that makes possible the achievement of the complex goals that Reggio educators have set for themselves.

Not a pre-set curriculum but a process of inviting and sustaining learning. Once teachers have prepared an environment rich in materials and possibilities, they observe and listen to the children in order to know how to proceed with their work. Teachers use the understanding they gain thereby to act as a resource for them. They ask questions and thus discover the children's ideas, hypotheses, and theories. They see learning not as a linear process but as a spiral progression and consider themselves to be partners in this process of learning. After observing children in action, they compare, discuss, and interpret together with other teachers their observations, recorded in different ways, to leave traces of what has been observed. They use their interpretations and discussions to make choices that they share with the children.

The power of documentation. Transcriptions of children's remarks and discussions, photographs of their activity, and representations of their thinking and learning are carefully studied. These documents have several functions. Most importantly, they help to determine the direction in which the work and experiences with the children will go. Once these documents are organized and displayed, they help to make parents aware of their children's experience and maintain their involvement. They make it possible for teachers to understand the children better and to evaluate the teachers' own work, thus promoting their professional growth; they make children aware that their effort is valued; and furthermore, they create an archive that traces the history of the school.

The many languages of children. *Atelierista* and atelier. A teacher with a background in the visual arts works closely with the other teachers and the children in every preprimary school and visits the infant/toddler centers. This teacher, who works in a special workshop or studio known as an atelier, is called an *atelierista*. The atelier contains a great variety of tools and resource materials, along with records of past projects and experiences. What is done with materials and media is not regarded as art per se, because in the view of Reggio educators the children's use of many media is not a separate part of the curriculum but an inseparable, integral part of the whole cognitive/symbolic expression involved in the process of learning.

Ochoa Early Childhood Studio,
Tucson, Arizona

Through time, the materials and work of the atelier has entered into all the classrooms through the setting up of "mini-ateliers," as teachers and *atelierista* learn to work in very connected ways.

Projects. Projects provide the narrative and structure to the children's and teachers' learning experiences. They are based on the strong conviction that learning by doing is of great importance and that to discuss in groups and to revisit ideas and experiences is essential to gain better understanding and to learn. Projects may start either from a chance event, an idea or a problem posed by one or more children, or an experience initiated directly by teachers. They can last from a few days to several months.

Educators in Reggio Emilia have no intention of suggesting that their program should be looked at as a model to be copied in other countries; rather, they consider their work as an educational experience that consists of reflection on theory, practice, and further careful reflection in a program that is continuously renewed and readjusted. Considering the enormous interest that educators show in the work done in the Reggio schools, they suggest that teachers and parents in each school, any school, anywhere, could in their own context reflect on these ideas, keeping in focus always the relationships and learning that are in process locally to examine needs and strengths, thus finding possible ways to construct change.[2]

The City of Reggio Emilia

*"When I came to visit Reggio Emilia,
invited to see its world-famous preschools,
I expected another "small city miracle."
But I was not prepared for what I found.*

*It was not just that they were better than
anything I had ever seen...
What struck me about the Reggio preschools
was how they cultivated imagination and,
in the process, how they empowered
the children's sense of what is possible."*[3]

JEROME BRUNER

Reggio Emilia, a small Italian city in the heart of
the economically prosperous Po River Valley of the
Emilia Romagna region, has developed within the
centuries-old tradition of cooperative agricultural
work. Talent, imagination, and professional skills
have been dedicated to young children as well. It is
the site of a most celebrated educational system.

Saturday afternoon, the central piazza of Reggio Emilia, with City Hall and the adjoining historic building where the first designed Italian flag was introduced to the citizens. A piazza, in Italian cities, is a space for social gatherings, business and weekly markets, children and families, political demonstrations, and celebrations.

From an Honorary Citizen of Reggio Emilia

Jerome Bruner

I've been making annual visits to Reggio Emilia since 1994 and, indeed, I feel by now that Reggio is my "second home." And a few years ago, I was much moved when the City Council there reciprocated by electing me a *cittadino onorario* to make me feel even more at home among them!

What keeps me coming back is not only my affection for the city and its ways, but the manner in which they conceive of education there. For my *Reggiani* colleagues—and for the children they teach—education is devoted not to a product but to a process. It is not about accumulating know-how or knowledge, but about how one uses mind and heart.

The first and most revolutionary principle in the Reggio approach is both that individuals are not, as it were, isolated one from the other, and that human sensibility is based on a sharing of minds and hearts in dialogue and interaction. Eating and enjoying lunch together is as crucial and educational an activity as learning, say, that the closer an object gets to a source of light, the larger the shadow it will cast. And both of these—lunch and "physics"—can be better understood and better enjoyed by honest discussion of one's thoughts and one's uncertainties.

What always delights me, visiting the *Reggiane* preschools, is the lively recognition that we don't "receive" knowledge by our exposure to the world, but that we "create" it by our way of thinking (and feeling) about what we are encountering. The teachers and the children come to accept this as a "way of life."

Let me return to the little example I mentioned of the shadows cast by objects as they are held up to a light. I remember a discussion at the Diana Scuola dell'Infanzia, I'll never forget it. One kid said, trying to explain why an object's shadow gets bigger as it gets closer to a source of light, "The shadow's trying to tell you something about how far apart things are." And another kid said, "Yeah, but it's really trying to tell you how much of the light that object is blocking off. If it blocks off ALL the light, everything will be shadow." Meanwhile, the teacher was saying things like, "Very interesting, does anybody have any other ideas about shadows?" We were all having a ball!

It was a discussion that could have taken place in a graduate school seminar on physics or in a nursery school in Reggio. You know: "What's a shadow, anyway?" But the kids were also recognizing that you can find out a lot by exchanging ideas about something mysterious with others. And maybe the latter was more important than the former!

The Reggio approach is dedicated to intellectual honesty and to interpersonal honesty. It is not easily summarized—nor are its results easily measured by conventional psychometric methods. I keep visiting Reggio to learn more, and I am never disappointed!

The Stone Lions,
Reggio Emilia

Section One

Loris Malaguzzi
Founder and Philosopher:
His Image of the Child

"One of our strong points has always been to start from an explicit declaration about the very open image of the child that we hold.

An image, in the sense of an interpretation, strong and optimistic about the child; a child who is born with many resources and extraordinary potentialities that never fail to surprise us; a child with autonomous capacities to construct thoughts, ideas, questions and attempts to give answers. (A child) who has high capacity to dialogue with the adult, to observe things and to reconstruct them entirely.

We see the child, every child, as a gifted child for whom there has to be a gifted teacher. This consideration has led us to the condition and also into the responsibility to always proceed with teachers unifying moments of theoretical research, of theoretical values, with the ones of practical experience." [1]

LORIS MALAGUZZI

Contributors

LELLA GANDINI tells us about the first dialogue between Loris Malaguzzi and one of the people who greatly influenced Malaguzzi's work, the philosopher of science David Hawkins.

BAJI RANKIN reports a conversation with Loris Malaguzzi concerning the recurrent debate about the source of growth and development of children's intelligence, which she had occasion to discuss with him during her long stay in Reggio Emilia.

BARBARA ACTON delves into the subject of her daily work: the care and education of children with special rights. She clarifies and tells how the powerful learning through the philosophy of Reggio Emilia helps educators to find resources, strength, and respectful support for the development of these children.

SUSAN FRASER analyses how educators in Reggio Emilia give teachers the possibility to reflect and take initiatives based on different ways of considering principles of inclusion. She discusses children who have challenges or who are just beginning their school experience, or parents who have their first experience with school or have cultural experiences different from the mainstream.

SUE BREDEKAMP analyzes Malaguzzi's rich ability to create and use metaphors in his mission to transform the educator's view of the child, of teaching, and of learning. She bases her observations on her first encounter with Loris Malaguzzi, when she visited the preschools of Reggio, her visits that followed, and her close reading of Malaguzzi's writing.

"Shortly after the conclusion of the Second World War, a young journalist named Loris Malaguzzi, who was living in Reggio, happened to visit a small bombed village near the town and was deeply moved by the experience. Having studied pedagogy, he decided to remain in the Reggio area and to attempt to create good schools for young children.

Over the next decades, he worked tirelessly and imaginatively with a growing cadre of committed young educators to launch and improve a group of schools for infants (from under a year old to three years old) and for preschoolers (three to six years old). In the early 1990s, Newsweek *declared that the preschools of Reggio were the best in the world. In general I place little stock in such ratings, but here I concur. The twenty-two municipal preschools and thirteen infant-and-toddler day care centers and preschools in this charmed community are unique."*[2]

HOWARD GARDNER

Meeting of Minds Malaguzzi and Hawkins

Lella Gandini

Loris Malaguzzi always said that the sources of his learning were essentially two: first of all, his experiences of observing and working with children and teachers; and second, the extraordinary range of ideas that he, an indefatigable and eclectic reader, absorbed from books and articles on the latest research in child development, science, philosophy and the arts, and that nourished and energized his imagination and creativity. When asked, he would reel off the names of several noted authors in various fields whom he credited with informing and inspiring his work. Always prominent among these was the American philosopher of science and education David Hawkins, in whose collection of essays, *The Informed Vision*, one can readily see how Loris was drawn to and inspired by the author's sharp intelligence and thus understand how compatible the meeting of those two minds was.

When Loris first came to the University of Massachusetts in 1988 for the opening of The Hundred Languages of Children exhibit and stayed in our home, he was very surprised to learn that my husband and I were friends of David Hawkins and even more that David was still alive. I personally recognized this tendency to consider somebody famous, admired, and met only through reading as living only in the past.

We called David then and there, using the speakerphone and, as he spoke Italian, we witnessed the most amazing conversation between the two of them, each so surprised by this spontaneous encounter and admiring of the other. Once Loris overcame his disbelief, he managed to invite David to Reggio Emilia. Eventually David visited Reggio twice: once for the very first large-scale international conference, held in 1990, and then in 1992 to observe in the schools there together with his wife, Frances, herself a noted expert on early childhood education.

In the accompanying image we see the two philosophers together engaged with children. Both believed in the importance of seeing children's processes of learning through action and also of renewing oneself with an open mind. Upon such a common base each was able to learn from the other. Loris, for example, drew on David's insights into the competence of children in solving problems when encouraging teachers to be observant. With this message, I wish to recognize the value and power of such an exchange of ideas, especially when they come, as Loris used to say, "from beautiful heads."

Children keep watch over a Malaguzzi - Hawkins checkers match at La Villetta School, Reggio Emilia

Theoretical Debate Whether Intelligence Grows from a Social Situation or from Inside Every Child

Baji Rankin

The following conversation with Loris Malaguzzi took place in June 1990 in the city of Reggio Emilia. Speaking of working with children in small groups, Malaguzzi said:

> *What you most easily see is the development, I would say, of socializing and sociability of children through accommodation and cooperation. What you see less, but what inevitably happens, according to more or less favorable conditions, is intellectual growth that the children attain working among themselves. It is the development of intelligence in situations like this that has not yet been sufficiently explored...*

> *The theoretical dispute is among those who sustain that intelligence grows from a social situation and those who say that intelligence grows inside every child seen in some way separated or disconnected from other children. This is what exists on the level of theoretical debate...Therefore, I believe, the development of sociability, of a social exchange, and of intelligence necessarily happens in a social situation.*

> *It's not so much that we need to think of a child who develops himself by himself but rather of a child who develops himself interacting and developing with others.*

> *A determining contribution to children's construction of knowledge, we believe, is the involvement of the adult, not only because the adult legitimizes children's curiosity and knowledge, but also because the adult values and addresses children's investigations and suggestions with supports and suggestions as well.*

The powerful words and ideas that Malaguzzi expresses in this conversation have stayed with me in my work with children and teachers since that time. Malaguzzi challenged educators to develop new eyes to truly see the intelligence of children, bringing attention to the value of observing and documenting children's learning. The issues Malaguzzi identified are relevant and essential today for teachers who want to work from a deep understanding of children's thinking and questions.

Roberta, teacher at Anna Frank Preschool, and five-year-old children during the Dinosaur Project.

Children with Special Rights

Barbara Acton

I believe the Reggio Emilia philosophy offers us many gifts. Among these gifts are a strong image of every child and the belief that schools should be for all children, not based on the conviction that they are all the same, but rather that they are all different. Perhaps most importantly, our friends in Reggio have inspired in us a desire to want to know more, to create schools as places of relationships and learning, and to embrace a pedagogical approach that is open to possibilities. Reggio inspires us to want schools that are places of care and education, with a commitment to observe, document, and reflect, so that we may truly know children.

To explain my feelings and work related to inclusion, I need to briefly tell about my life experiences, for they necessarily influence my thoughts and ideas, my perceptions and knowledge. I am one of six children; I have three sisters and two brothers. Though labor and delivery differed for each of us, and ten years separated my oldest sister from my youngest brother, we were all born full term and each was identified as a "healthy baby" at birth. Prior to going to school, we spent countless hours playing house, building forts, and transforming the treasures in our backyard into magic potions and ice cream. We loved swimming, playing with neighborhood friends, catching lightning bugs, riding bikes, and listening to bedtime stories.

When two of my sisters started school, their days of imaginative play and creative problem-solving were devastatingly altered. Schools then, and too often today, were structured to give answers, not ask questions; to focus on teaching, not learning; and, to emphasize telling, not listening. My sisters, like all children, were rich with capabilities, ideas, curiosity, and wonder, but unfortunately, because of perceived language delays and difficulties unlocking the mysteries and wonders of print, they were identified and labeled as slow, delayed, and learning disabled. Thus began an educational journey that often separated, alienated, and isolated them from their peers. The historically typical practices of pull-out therapies, resource-room learning, and the push by many to "just try harder" created great angst and self-doubt within both of my sisters.

It was their experiences that compelled me to want to become a teacher and what later drew me to the Reggio Emilia philosophy. I wanted to make a positive difference. I wanted to be a source of hope, a partner in learning who did not blame or shame the child and family but, rather, embraced and loved each unique child. I chose a university for my undergraduate degree that would allow me to major in both elementary and special education.

My first teaching experience was in a public school working with children with special learning needs in kindergarten through second grade. By mid-year, I was troubled to have witnessed and been part of numerous Individualized Education Plan (IEP) conferences in which the school's educational psychologist systematically and without emotion described children not by quoting ideas they had shared or relating stories of relationships they had developed and challenges they had worked through, but by listing test score after test score, including the child's IQ, that would qualify the child for special support: "standard deviations," "below average," "areas of deficiency." I ask all of us as educators to be conscious of the language and methods we use to describe children in the context of education. Do they potentially open doors or close doors?

Our colleagues in Reggio Emilia offer us words, images, and metaphors: a competent child; a pedagogy of listening; the hundred languages of children; children with special rights.

Language has a profound effect on our thinking and our imaginations. As we are reminded again and again by our friends in Reggio, our image of the child is where our teaching begins. For a few moments, picture in your mind a child, any child. Hold that image as you read the words of Loris Malaguzzi.

The child
is made of one hundred.
The child has
a hundred languages
a hundred hands
a hundred thoughts
a hundred ways of thinking
of playing, of speaking.
A hundred always a hundred
ways of listening
of marveling
of loving
a hundred joys
for singing and understanding
a hundred worlds
to discover
a hundred worlds
to invent
a hundred worlds
to dream.
The child has a hundred languages
(and a hundred hundred more).[3]

A story of Michael and Ramya

The sequence of photographs on these pages tells you a story about two children in our program. Michael is a child with Down syndrome. He began attending our center as a toddler. This past year he was among the children in our first fully inclusive class. Ramya also began attending the center as a toddler. She has been diagnosed with microcephaly and cortical visual impairment. Both have learned to walk with the assistance of physical therapists and benefit from the assistance of adaptive equipment to develop fine motor skills. All of the children know and love Ramya and Michael, and love to make Ramya laugh. Her teachers joyfully shared the story of the morning in circle when the children noticed Ramya laugh when someone sneezed, and longing to hear her laughter again, one by one the children all pretended to sneeze in hopes that Ramya might laugh once more. From the first day of school this year, Michael has shown a special interest in Ramya and a growing affection. He has been a keen observer and sought ways—not always comfortably received by Ramya—to be "close to her" to express his affection. And yet both persisted. Through the observations and documentation of their teachers, we can give value to their progress and to their trying.

The motivation to try is important. The awareness of the children is important. The pleasure of the children is important. These images of Ramya and Michael embody a vision of children with special needs that is rich and powerful, does not limit and, in the words of Malaguzzi, "does not separate the head from the body."

As you look at the images of Michael and Ramya, I invite you to think about an educational approach that values relating, knowing, and loving—an educational approach that recognizes and gives value to "the hundred languages of children" and the verbs *to connect, to listen, to exchange*. Many have noted the demands of oppressive standards and testing that more and more impact our daily lives with our children in schools, and the narrow definitions of what is good, what is normal. If these are the standards to be applied to all of us, to define what is of value, what do these "standards" say about the worth and value of a child with special needs? No wonder families are resistant to our labels, to special services. The time to act is now. The time to be courageous and strong is now.

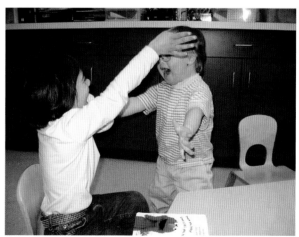

Loris Malaguzzi told us that in the beginning they all knew one important thing: they didn't know enough. When we are able to commit ourselves as adults, as educators who are learners with questions, and embrace our roles as researchers, then we may know each child and together open doors of possibility. We will not limit them, and thus, we will not limit humanity or ourselves. For a child with special rights this is particularly important because we and society have a tendency to know them first, sometimes only, by their narrowly defined characteristics and/or symptoms of their diagnosis. Though it is true that children with different medical conditions, such as Down syndrome, often share certain characteristics, each child sees and experiences the world very differently. To know Maddie, a child in our program with Down syndrome, is to know that she loves horses, bubble baths, the color purple, and singing. To know Christopher, another child with Down syndrome, is to know that one of his first sounds was "ger" as he pointed to Tigger, and that he loves to play with his brother, Nicholas.

Loris Malaguzzi's wisdom teaches us that "children are a wealth of resources. If we limit them we limit ourselves."

If we are able to see our children/all children (the visible and the invisible) as "rich with humanity," capable of complex thinking, and as made of "one hundred languages, and a hundred hundred more," and if we are able to create schools that recognize and give value to young children's ideas, inquiry, and learning, then we, as Carlina Rinaldi has so poignantly reminded us, must begin with the questions: Who is a child? How does a child know and learn? And what is the role of the adult?

Our colleagues in Reggio have reminded us that from the first day of life children are capable of communicating, long before speaking a word. Children communicate with their eyes, their expressions, and their gestures, and they have an innate desire to connect, to be in relationship with the world. They are capable and expressive, with or without the potential to communicate with words.

This includes children with profound medical conditions—children who in the United States are often referred to as children with special needs but in Reggio are referred to as children with special rights. How powerful the shift to refer to the child as having special rights rather than special needs. To focus on a child's needs only, we risk limiting them, we risk not truly knowing them. The child within the child with special needs may not be discovered, may not be known. It is like the blind mice trying to identify the elephant but only exploring one part.

If instead, we ask ourselves, Who is this unique child? we will not limit the child and we will enrich ourselves. We must be willing to ask, What does it mean to be a boy, a girl, and who is this child, this boy or girl? Then we may remember that all children desire relationships with others and with the world. And we can remember that all children are creative and have potentials for communicating with multiple languages.

When we ask, Who is this child? we are also better able to know and value that no two children are exactly alike. I am the mother of identical twin sons: This is to say that they have the exact same DNA, the same genetic makeup, and were separated at birth by less than a minute—and yet they are very different people. Why if "identical twins" are very different, do we create schools and pedagogy based on the belief that they, children, three-year-olds, four-year-olds, five-year-olds, are all the same and that they need the same thing at the same time in order to be "ready" for kindergarten? Or that we celebrate the passing of each season the same way every year? I appreciate very much that our friends in Reggio give value to an educational approach that is about learning as life and is a journey with unexpected surprises. Their approach in my opinion *promotes a shift of focus from teaching to learning, from telling to listening, from answers to questions.*

Widening the Principles of Inclusion through Relationship

Susan Fraser

The educators in Reggio Emilia have been instrumental in shifting the image of the child from a child with needs that adults strive to meet to a child with strengths that adults recognize and support. As a result, adults who embrace the Reggio Emilia approach view children as producers of the culture as opposed to consumers of resources.

This image of the child means that children have the right to the highest quality early childhood education. This shift in image has had a powerful impact on the education of children who are challenged in one or more areas of development. It has forced educators to think carefully about inclusion and how they can provide children with disabilities (in Reggio called "children with special rights") with an education that enables them to reach their full potential.

In considering the Reggio Emilia approach, teachers begin to understand how the principles of inclusion can have a wider scope in early childhood education. If teachers agree with the educators from Reggio Emilia, they will review every aspect of their programs to strengthen and make relationship the foundation of the program.

Let us, as teachers, consider briefly the relationships we have with families in terms of inclusion. The initial contact with families will set the tone for future relationships between home and school. The educators in Reggio Emilia believe that beginnings or *inserimento* (transition) are critical. The initial interactions between parents, children, and teachers set the pattern of all future interactions, communication, and reciprocal relations. In Reggio Emilia, the transition from home to school is considered part of the cycle of exchange that goes beyond the entry of the child to school. The child's transition from home to school is considered part of a widening circle of relationships whereby the child and family become a part of the school and community. This is why it is important that enough time is provided so that families begin to feel welcome even before children enter the school.

It is essential that clear expectations are communicated to families through written materials and verbal interactions. Documentation displayed, for instance, in the entryway of the school can be used to show examples of ways parents can participate in the program. Documentation displayed on panels, in portfolios, or vignettes sent by e-mail informs the parents about their child's experiences in school.

In our experience in British Columbia, teachers realized the importance of listening and communicating honestly with parents, knowing that open communication is possible only when trust has been established. The teachers planned creative ways to involve parents in the program beyond doing the essential jobs of serving on committees and driving the children on field trips. For instance, they offered parents the opportunity to participate in projects in which the children were involved.

The teachers tried to accommodate differences in values with families, knowing that these might block communication between school and family. They realized that they needed to keep the door of communication not only open, but wide open.

Loris Malaguzzi stated: "Of course, education is not based solely on relationships; however, we consider relationship to be the fundamental, organizing strategy of our educational system. We view relationship not simply as a warm protective backdrop or blanket but as a coming together of elements interacting dynamically toward a common purpose. The strength of this view of education is in expanding the forms and functions of relationship and interaction."[4]

As early childhood educators, therefore, we thought to reassess "the form and function" that relationship plays in our program by asking the following questions:

Are we engaging in culturally sensitive interaction with the families in the center?

Are we supportive and able to make families that are under stress feel that they still can be involved in the program?

Are we exploring ways of involving all families in the program?

Are we including the richness of the community in the program?

Are we making clear the options that are available for families to participate in the program?

Have we established reciprocity as a core principle in our relationship with families?

Malaguzzi's Metaphors The Power of Imagery to Transform Educational Practice and Policy

Sue Bredekamp

Recently, in reviewing research on how people learn, I was not surprised to find that creating metaphors is among the most effective teaching strategies. For many years, I have reflected on the power of the Reggio Emilia approach, not just as it functions so well in Italy with children, teachers, and families, but how it has influenced thinking and practice in widely diverse cultures throughout the world.

Loris Malaguzzi was a poet. Given the difficulty of translating complex concepts into multiple languages and across widely varying social and cultural contexts, I long ago credited Malaguzzi's metaphors as the beginning of a process that successfully communicated the Reggio Emilia approach to the world. Carlina Rinaldi said it best in *Making Learning Visible*: "We have a great love of metaphor; and this is primarily because children love and often make use of it...Metaphorical language, precisely because it is more undefined, allusive, and sometimes ambiguous, but at the same time open to new concepts, becomes the only tool available to the new understanding that is seeking to emerge and find an audience." [5]

Most obviously, the hundred languages of children—the dominant metaphor of the Reggio Emilia approach—communicates in five words what would require five volumes of discourse to convey what those educators have learned about children, their capacities, and this particularly powerful way of educating them. On his visit to Washington, DC, in 1993, Malaguzzi admitted that when they started with the "hyperbolic idea of one hundred languages," they were engaging in "sly public relations, but the words were more true than truth itself. Now, they would say children have one thousand languages." He went on to say, "Our fear is that children have the chance to use only twenty of these languages."

During my first visit to Reggio in 1993, like others, I took away images of the documentation of projects and the aesthetically beautiful schools. "Project" is itself a metaphor—definite and indefinite at the same time—taking action into the realm of uncertainty on the part of both the children and teachers, with the child inside the process and the process advancing through co-construction, conflict, and negotiation.

But even more lasting for me have been the images created by Malaguzzi's metaphors. Describing the fact that in most schools today children use only part of their potential, Malaguzzi said, "The child can't have a piano with twenty keys. He needs the piano of Mozart! But it is necessary that the teacher knows every note—an octave above and one below,

48 SECTION ONE

which notes are harmonious and which are not. Every note has its own sounds, strength, color, vibration." When one North American delegate inquired in typical linear fashion, "Are the notes the children or the activities?" Malaguzzi loudly clapped his hands together (getting everyone's attention on that warm June afternoon) and vigorously explained, "The child does not exist without materials. When talking here, we are always putting things together." The image of his hands together remains vivid in my mind all these years hence, along with the metaphor of the piano.

Reggio's pedagogy of listening is perhaps the most difficult metaphor for traditional educators to grasp. "Talking to children requires three eyes," Malaguzzi said, describing listening as the most important action. The reciprocity required for co-construction depends on openness and the ability to listen, understanding that the other person gives meaning to my speech. The power of such communication is evident in one of my favorite metaphors of the work of Reggio Emilia schools: "the place theory and practice touch like the magic moment when night becomes day."

Section Two

A Renewed Image of the Teacher

Carlina Rinaldi and Amelia Gambetti

Contributors

Carol Brunson Day asserts that teachers from diverse communities can create and recreate their own educational space once they are empowered to consider themselves as creators.

Rebecca S. New focuses on the image of the adult, both teacher and parent, and the relationships that they construct in their work to support young children's well-being and learning.

David Kelly writes about his transformation as a teacher when he began to see the children for what they could be rather than being limited by the routine of the school day.

Mary Beth Radke reflects on the importance of sharing one's doubts and questions with her colleague Amelia Gambetti in order to become better able to observe the children with a keen and attentive eye.

Mary Mindess recalls the first Reggio-inspired Institute Day at Lesley University in 1993. She discusses the importance and potential of such institutes in inspiring change in early childhood communities, and highlights in particular Al Bustan, a bilingual preschool for Muslim families in Cambridge, Massachusetts.

Carol Bersani, Becky Fraizer, and Carolyn Galizio tell a poetic story of children's collaborative problem-solving to highlight the supportive role of the teacher as observer and co-inquirer.

Beth MacDonald discusses how she integrates harmonically the two philosophies of Montessori and Reggio Emilia in her school, while describing their similarities and differences. Next, Sandy Burwell, *atelierista*, and Audrey Favorito, a parent, tell about two four-year-old children who invent a story about butterflies so rich that, with the help of the teachers, it becomes a film.

Margie Carter and Deb Curtis respond to what they determine to be the greatest gift and the biggest challenge Reggio has given us: a sense of hope and possibility for transformation.

Simonetta Cittadini-Medina, in a letter to Amelia Gambetti, describes the development of understanding of the Reggio values in her school, L'Atelier, and in her own self as educator. She also asks three teachers in her school about their views on the concept of quality. Although each teacher has a different view, all three consider how the search for quality impacts their work.

Loris Malaguzzi was once asked this question:

You said that teachers should also be researchers. How do you promote that?

Here is his response:

"To learn and relearn together with children is our line of work…There are two ways in which we can look into children's learning processes and find clues for supporting them. One is the way children enter into an activity and develop their strategies of thought and action; the other is the way in which the objects involved are transformed…Our teachers do research either on their own or with their colleagues to produce strategies that favor children's work or can be utilized by them. They go from research into action (or vice versa). When all teachers in the school are in agreement, the projects, strategies, and styles of work become intertwined and the school becomes a truly different school.

"Some of our teachers proceed in this research with more intentionality and better methods than others; the records and documentaries that result from their endeavors are significant beyond the immediate needs of action and become common objects of study, at times with so much substance as to become of interest to a wider audience. As a result, these teachers feel, and help others feel, more motivation to grow and attain a much higher level of professionalism. In the process, our teachers realize that they must avoid the temptation of expecting children to give them back what they already know, but instead they must retain the same sense of wonder that children live through their discoveries."[1]

Carlina Rinaldi has written that Loris Malaguzzi always asked to start from the children to reformulate the role of the teacher and learner in the educational process. Carlina: "Malaguzzi felt that teachers have the task of giving orientation, meaning, and value to the experience of schools and children. Teachers are the ones who construct and constitute the interweaving and connections, the web of relationships, in order to transform them in significant experiences of interactions and communications."[2]

Teacher as Creator

Carol Brunson Day

In a 2004 interview for Innovations *magazine, I was asked the question, "What from the Reggio approach has important implications for work in diverse communities in the United States?"*

Carol Brunson Day's granddaughter

I believe that one of the most powerful Reggio principles is that the teacher is a creator, not an imitator. The teacher neither reproduces what others have done nor reproduces year after year what she herself has done in the past. Rather, the teacher, as one of many parts that form the relationship they call "school," actively stimulates new creations. That is, the school itself is much more than a building or a place—by definition, it is a relationship that exists as a consequence of interactions among children, families, and teachers. The interactions among these people are what make the school and, in turn, what make the curriculum. So the school gets created and recreated with every group that participates. It is alive and changing, making and remaking itself.

I find this idea very empowering for disenfranchised communities—to be regarded as places that create and recreate their own schools; to be thought about as not having to copy or imitate others, but as having the innate and natural ability to become and be a school, unique and individual with its own personality. Each teacher then is empowered in the process—challenged and empowered—to construct curriculum that builds together with the children and families in a deeply personal way. For me it is truly respectful of the individual child within the context of her family, her community, and her culture.

New Ways of Looking at Roses and Relationships
Provocations from Reggio Emilia

Rebecca S. New

Yes, a rose is a rose is a rose, but what about a whole bunch of roses? A gift of love, remembrance, celebration? A gardener's pride? Or, perhaps, the source of pale pink petals? Reggio Emilia's capacity to deconstruct the taken-for-granted and reveal that which often goes unseen might well be symbolized by this image, captured when I spent a week in the *Scuola Diana* in 1992. I remember being struck by the simple beauty of the rose petals in the recycled plastic tray next to a glass bowl, each proposing a new way to look at familiar objects. I have used this image multiple times since then as an example of Reggio Emilia's attention to environmental aesthetics. Sometimes I have interpreted it as a metaphor for Reggio's image of the child: beautiful, surprising, and not nearly as fragile or predictable as appearances might suggest. I now use this image to represent yet another feature, delicate but central to the promise offered by Reggio Emilia's example—the primacy of **adult** relationships as means and ends of its work with young children.

Reggio Emilia's collaborative and communal orientation to the care and education of young children is not unique in Italy. The neighbor city Parma has used the phrase *"la qualita come relazione"* (quality as relationships) to describe and celebrate that community's three decades of infant/toddler services. More recently, I have used the phrase "not-for-children-only" to describe *servizi dell'infanzia* in cities such as Milan, Parma, Trento, Pistoia, and San Miniato as they support the purposeful engagement of parents and other community members in their various municipal early childhood services. What is particular to Reggio Emilia is the effort put into insuring that these relationships—among children, teachers, families, and other members of the community—are reciprocal, enduring, and endearing. And these qualities are interpreted in ways not always consistent with prevailing norms within educational settings elsewhere. Among the dozens of personal memories, the following give voice and color to Reggio Emilia's philosophy of **schools as systems of relations** translated into everyday *praxis*.

We don't argue enough anymore. It was the summer of 1987. We had spent the morning at the Reggio Emilia school La Villetta—I was with a small group of students from Syracuse University, likely the first U.S. preservice early childhood teachers to ever visit Reggio Emilia. As the children played outside, the adults took a break in one of the classrooms, indulging in Italian biscotti, glasses of *aranciata* (Italian orange soda) and, for me, an espresso. We learned that the two teachers had taught together for seventeen years. I marveled at the presumed closeness of their friendship after all those years, only to have Amelia (yes, *the* Amelia Gambetti) explain that they had requested new assignments for the coming year.

I was embarrassed, assuming that I had assumed
too much about the quality of their relationship.
But then Amelia explained. "We need to move to
separate classes because we don't argue enough
anymore." It was at this point that I began to realize
that Reggio Emilia's interpretations of good
professional relationships with colleagues did not
correspond to the dominant definition.

Subsequent to that visit, I have observed Reggio Emilia teachers hundreds of times as they skillfully utilize the benefits of socio-cognitive conflict to ensure the presence of multiple and alternative perspectives, to maintain intellectual alertness to previously unimagined hypotheses, and to avoid the dulling passivity often associated with a quest for consensus. Back in the United States, it remains difficult to imagine most teachers welcoming such an orientation to their professional conversations, much less their relationships. But few can argue with the apparent benefits. Even among parents.

Of course we have conflicts. You can't have a relationship without conflicts. This statement was made by a parent participant in our research project. The question was one of several designed to elicit information about the quality of home-school relations in Italian early childhood services. The response revealed an aspect of the highly touted parent-teacher relationship that consistently evokes surprise when shared with American early childhood educators. Within the United States, a pervasive lack of confidence in parents as knowledgeable contributors to children's early development has historically served as a rationale for early childhood programs. This deficit view of parents has also informed programs dedicated to the professional development of teachers. The formation of the National Council of Parental Education in 1928 gave voice and vocabulary to the premise that parents know less and experts know

more about children and their development. By the 1940s, the utility of research on child development for children's early care and education was well established; and the 1950s saw increasing numbers of mothers as consumers of parent education manuals. The primacy of scientific validation was the basis for the National Association for the Education of Young Children's published guidelines for developmentally appropriate practice.[3] In contrast, Reggio Emilia's accomplishments with young children are the results of their approach to collaborative inquiry and a willingness to include parents as partners in planning and evaluating children's early educational experiences. The inclusion of adults other than teachers as active decision-makers is not limited to immediate family members.

Why shouldn't I be here? I am a citizen of the community. This is important. Italian interpretations of a democratic society include notions of civic engagement that demand much more of its citizens than merely showing up at the polls. Drawing upon decades of activism heightened by the sense of purpose following World War II, Italians have repeatedly demonstrated their willingness to take a stand on a wide range of controversial topics associated with women's status in contemporary society as well as the early care and education of children, ranging from maternity leave and abortion rights to the reassignment of educational services for five-year-olds to the mandatory elementary school system.

Teachers and *atelieristi* in the Diana School

There is likely no city in Italy that has so successfully utilized that country's notion of civic engagement, or *partecipazione*, as Reggio Emilia. The power of this principle has been illustrated many times, most often as I observed meetings at the Comune when parents and other citizens advocate and vote on expenditures associated with early childhood services.

Parent, child, and teacher

The point became most visible, however, when attending an evening meeting at one of Reggio Emilia's *scuole dell'infanzia*. The room was filled with parents—mothers as well as fathers—and a few grandparents. We had been together for several hours as teachers presented insights and questions emerging from recent *progettazione*, when we took a break to enjoy Lambrusco wine and pound cake made with olive oil.

As the adults rose from their seats and turned to greet each other, I smiled at the forty-something man in the finely cut three-piece suit and asked, "What class is your child in?" He responded, "I don't have any children in this school." My surprise was surely noticeable: "Then why are you here?" (at this hour, I wanted to add, since it was approaching midnight). But his next response was the one that I will never forget: "I'm a citizen of Reggio Emilia. Child care is important."

It is no accident that Reggio Emilia has managed to secure persistently high levels of funding for the city's integrated services for children from birth through age six. Much has been written about the purposeful use of documentation to keep parents and community members informed of children's vast learning capacities, the frequent journeys into public spaces to remind community members of their youngest citizens, and the powerful advocacy of such spokespersons as Loris Malaguzzi, Sergio Spaggiari, and Carlina Rinaldi on behalf of their work with young children. And yet I am convinced that the success of Reggio Emilia is largely dependent on the quality and nature of the individual relationships that have been nurtured on a daily basis among and between teachers, family members, and other citizens of this community.

Of all the things for which I am most grateful to Reggio Emilia, it is this image of adults as having the potential and the responsibility to ask better questions of ourselves and each other. Reggio Emilia has challenged our ethical imaginations to consider the benefits to children and communities if we, too, were to acknowledge our shared responsibility, appreciate our diverse perspectives, and work harder at listening to and learning from one another.

Encounters with Reggio

David Kelly, Jr.

My first encounter with Reggio Emilia came when I met Loris Malaguzzi in Chicago some fifteen or so years ago, when he was receiving an award from the Kohl Foundation. To say this was a transformative experience would be an understatement in view of how much my life has changed since that day. Feeling smart and just out of art school, I was not prepared for what followed: I would make a decision to work with children in the inner city.

Part and parcel of this encounter meant finding the capacity to imagine, while seeing the possible as a reality from which you could begin. Loris Malaguzzi offered the opportunity to see children and the world for what they could be, which meant not living from the routine and mundane offering of the day to day. He cajoled us to live out our thinking and to think about how we live in relationship to the world around us. It was, as I recall, both an illustration of what we take for granted and a celebration at the same time. A year later, I encountered Reggio Emilia, the place. This was like being provoked by Loris Malaguzzi all over again.

When I visited the Loris Malaguzzi Center, the Ray of Light Atelier, and REMIDA*, I saw even more ways to participate with intention. Knowing these spaces exist as places of the possible and that they honor my own potential, I carry within myself a constant reminder of the need to create the same possibility: a place where we can all go to school, to find pleasure and joy in learning and being together, right where I live. In recollection, on that first day of meeting Loris Malaguzzi, I discovered a commitment to my life's work.

*REMIDA: The Creative Recycling Center. The development of REMIDA corresponds to the development of the atelier, and to the expression of languages through materials. In setting up this special recycling center, the guiding principles were creativity and ecology, encouraging an appreciation for the potential and beauty of materials. From the beginning, this special project and place was planned not only for children but also for adults, starting with teachers but including all the people of the city. The evolution of REMIDA has been natural because of the relationships that have developed among the different sectors of the Reggio community: school, industry, social services, and the world of culture.[4]

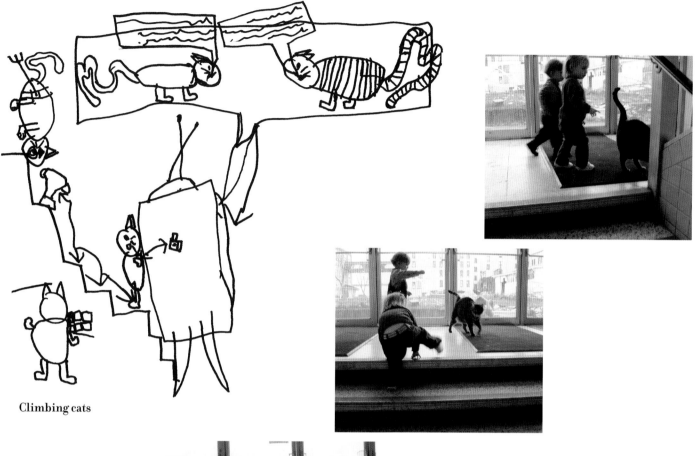

Climbing cats

Several children from the toddler room make their journey up to the third floor of the public school that houses the recycled materials in a room called the Hive.

Their excitement is palpable; the children know they are going to make discoveries with materials. This anticipation is heightened by finding Stripes the cat, who lives in the large atelier, sitting in the sun.

Curiosity, Doubts, Questions, and Observations

Mary Beth Radke

Curiosity nourished the experience that Amelia Gambetti and I had at the University of Massachusetts Laboratory Preschool in 1992–1993. What could happen if a teacher from Reggio Emilia joined a group of children and a teacher in the United States for an extended period of time? Nothing like this had been tried.

As for the two of us, we had a lot of doubts, but at the same time insisted on the right to observe the situation even while tentatively observing each other. From the doubts and observations, we framed questions. Did the routines, opportunities, environment, and interactions support a sense of well-being and discovery? Some of the questions were deeper: Who are we? For whose benefit are we here? Where do we come from? What do we want to do? How and why and for whom?

Answers to questions like these could not be found in guidelines or textbooks. We needed something that was not preconceived because this was a particular situation where children and circumstances were evolving. The children, together as a group for the first time, were from different countries (many did not speak English), and Amelia and I were together as teachers for the first time (we did not know each other). I came to appreciate that there is more than one truth or solution to every issue, especially if you trust and use your own mind. We chose paths that we discovered by actively observing the quantity and quality of relationships between children, children and materials, children and teachers, and teachers and parents. Keeping a trace of children's words and creations supported these observations. There was also the precious discovery that our growing friendship, which led to an energized way of working and conversing, would be significant not only in creating a unique and positive experience, but in bringing us joy.

That year together convinced us that yes, we could build a better sense of belonging, offer children new and significant possibilities for discovering their potential, and deepen connections for everyone in the school. It could happen here in the United States, in close collaboration with a teacher from Reggio Emilia. It was a beginning.

Amelia Gambetti at the University of Massachusetts Laboratory Preschool, 1992–93.

When Two Cultures Meet

Mary Mindess

The year was 1993. The Lesley University auditorium was abuzz with conversation as 200 early childhood educators eagerly awaited the beginning of their "Guided Journey into the Schools of Reggio Emilia." Many had read about this very effective approach in *Newsweek* magazine. Some had seen The Hundred Languages of Children exhibit. They all had many questions, but none truly anticipated where this journey would lead.

Lella Gandini, Amelia Gambetti, Giovanni Piazza, and Baji Rankin guided the group on the initial leg of the journey and presented many vivid images along the way. In this and in subsequent presentations, these educators and their colleagues clearly emphasized the schools as a reflection of the culture in which they exist. The message from Italian educators was, "We are pleased to share what works in our culture. It is up to you to determine adaptations for your own setting." Lesley University, located in Cambridge, Massachusetts, offered and continues to offer Reggio-inspired annual institutes.[5]

This challenge came at a very opportune time for American educators. In early childhood education, a strong polemic was developing with the developmentalists on one side and the proponents of achievement testing and measurable outcomes on the other. The developmentalists needed to rethink their arguments. The provocations presented in the discussions of the Reggio approach provided the stimulus for this process.

The discussions provided a deeper understanding of the image of the child and the power of aesthetically pleasing and purposefully structured environments. These discussions served to heighten teachers' self-reflection. What does it mean for teaching practices when the adults believe that the young child is a capable and competent human being? How is this deepening image of the child reflected in teacher-child interactions? What does co-construction of knowledge look like? How does collaboration impact learning? These questions guide the investigative journey as early childhood educators from the two cultures continue to meet and interact with each other. Reflecting on these questions has set the stage for deep and enduring change in early childhood practices in the United States and worldwide.

Following is a story that shows how this change is taking place in one school community. For many years, our Italian colleagues have been providing leadership through inspiration. Leading through inspiration is one the most powerful approaches to making a difference in the lives of others. Our colleagues from Reggio Emilia have inspired us to look at our own practices and to be in charge of our own transformations and growth. The following story describes the transformation process.

The setting for the story is Al Bustan, a bilingual preschool in Cambridge, Massachusetts. The children and adults who make up the school community include Marietta Sbraccia, staff developer in the Cambridge Literacy Project;

Mervat Zaghbul, Director of Al Bustan and Malik Academy; Tazeeya Syed, the classroom teacher; and the children and their parents.

Marietta Sbraccia attended several previous Reggio-inspired annual institutes and enrolled in one of the institutes for course credit. Following the institute, Marietta invited me, as the Lesley University professor responsible for the course, to visit one of the schools at which she was serving as a Cambridge literacy project consultant. Marietta, the school staff, and I had the following conversation about the experiences at the school.

MARY MINDESS: The paper that you wrote for the class included a drawing of a chrysanthemum on the cover. I was struck by this illustration and the accompanying poem. Tell me a bit about it.

MARIETTA: My original inspiration came from observing an actual pine cone in a workshop at the institute. I studied the pinecone, made a clay replica of it. Then I began to think of other things in nature that had similar unfolding properties. That's when I thought of the similarities to children's development.

As I reflected on the weekend at Lesley, I wondered how the concept of the atelier could fit into the systems in which I worked. I realized that the pinecone that I had chosen for my clay construction was now a metaphor for the direction I needed to think more about. Helping to make the child visible was my goal.

Gradation from

Closed to openness

Tightness to looseness

Shapes within shapes

Connected, visible

Organized and integrated

Through nature we can

Learn about the atelier

MARIETTA M. SBRACCIA

Muzn's before and after pictures

MARY: The teachers and I had been talking about this idea at our weekly meeting, but implementation seemed a long way off. The day after the institute I was scheduled to visit Al Bustan. Help me to understand more about the school environment at Al Bustan.

MARIETTA: Al Bustan is a school for Muslim families. English for most is a second language; the age of the children is from 2.9 to 3.9 years. Most of the activities have been whole group, formal instruction, and teacher directed. The teachers care deeply about the children. They are dedicated to their work. They work hard and love what they do. They are committed to understanding how children learn and providing the best possible education for them.

MARY: How did you help these teachers come to appreciate the value of listening for children's ideas and building on them?

MARIETTA: These are ideas we have been pondering for a while. Just by coincidence, on the day following the institute when I came into the class, teacher Tazeeya greeted me with an unanticipated degree of enthusiasm.

TEACHER TAZEEYA: Marietta, we have a topic for an investigation! Last week we were singing the Bear Hunt song. Going over the bridge was a part of the song. Now the children and I have become so interested in bridges.

MARIETTA: I quickly took the teacher's lead. I gathered a group of children to find out what they knew or wanted to know about bridges.

TEACHER MERVAT: The children's background knowledge about bridges was very limited. During the next few days we brought in books and pictures about bridges. Since the school is within walking distance of the Charles River, we took the first opportunity we could to take the children over a bridge.

TEACHER TAZEEYA: At first we needed to give children language—Look! I see a big bridge with cars going over it and boats going under it. Do you think we can walk over the bridge?

MARIETTA: It took some back-and-forth dialogue for the children to learn the language. We continued to take pictures and read stories, and began to construct our knowledge.

The bridge investigation took place during a period of about three weeks. Children expressed their ideas through clay, blocks, and sand. This deepening understanding was reflected in their constructions and in their drawings.

MARY: How do you feel about the approach?

TEACHER TAZEEYA: We are learning so much. The children made so many interesting observations and asked engaging questions.

MARY: I recognize that many of your parents are interested in their children's academic success. How do you think the parents will feel about this approach?

TEACHER MERVAT: We did ask the parents. Many had no comments. Others commented: "I couldn't believe that my child at age 2.5 was getting these concepts. They were opening her mind more. She has started to be more aware. Yesterday when we passed the bridge, she commented on it." "I was amazed at the language. She is getting much more vocabulary for reading."

MARY: How do you as teachers feel about this approach?

TAZEEYA: Very amazing. I was so happy and thrilled. I never expected this kind of information from such young children. I didn't realize young children could learn so much. The words are so concrete in their minds. The children are excited. Their pictures are amazing.

Fahad's before and after pictures

"I Need to Paint the Blue Heron"

Carol Bersani, Becky Fraizer, and Carolyn Galizio

The children intently explore the wetlands just beyond the school. Over time, they find and come to know an elusive Great Blue Heron that lives there. Kristopher sets out to represent this bird at the easel. Andrew walks over, drawn by Kristopher's words and work. Andrew asks a question and looks closely at the painting on the easel. A conversation ensues and provides a glimpse into the deep desire of children to represent and share their ideas, questions, and feelings.

Early one morning, Kristopher (4.3 years) walks in to see another child painting a picture of the Great Blue Heron.

KRISTOPHER: I need to do that. I need to paint that Blue Heron too. *He paints silently.* Two necks! Oh man, what was I thinking?

Andrew (4.11 yrs) walks over.

ANDREW: Is that a joke?

KRISTOPHER: No, I need another piece of paper. I really want to paint him. *He paints silently.* More room. I need more room.

ANDREW: Kristopher, you put the wings on his head. That is not where they go.

KRISTOPHER: Well, maybe they could be down lower.

ANDREW: No, that's not it. You will have to change it.

Kristopher paints again.

ANDREW: I still can't see them very well, but they are in the right spot.

Inspired by our study of the Reggio Emilia philosophy, we seek to construct a school of research, making visible and connecting the passionate ideas of the child with the values and intent of the teacher and the strong desires of the family. Through collaborative study, listening and interpreting in new ways, this seemingly short story becomes a composition with many interwoven and complex meanings for us.

Kristopher's teacher carefully designs a context for learning. She watches closely, documents, and adds materials upon request. Kristopher uses paint to record a significant observation, a memory within an experience. Andrew shares his developing skills for reflection and critique as he works with Kristopher's intent. Observation becomes an integral force for teachers and children, giving visibility and accessibility to each other's thinking.

Families become co-inquirers with teachers and children, widening the circle of understanding. As Kristopher's mother studies his paintings of the Blue Heron, she expresses her amazement at Kristopher's abilities for recall and interpreting critique as help. "He has a determined spirit, and he is also able to learn from his friendships," she says.

To embrace a new point of view has become a central tenet of the way we live together in school.

Connecting, Combining, and Integrating Two Philosophies

Beth MacDonald

Our journey at MacDonald Montessori School has been to integrate two philosophies—Reggio and Montessori.

In our view, there are several points of intersection and connection between the Montessori philosophy and the Reggio philosophy. Both follow the child and enjoy a prepared environment; in fact, both see the environment as a third teacher. Both approaches promote and encourage aesthetically beautiful schools, indoors and out.

Connecting, combining, and integrating the two philosophies has always been our focus, but now we are digging into the heart of the issue in terms of the role of the adult and the development of the classroom. I think we are now in the commitment phase, but this is difficult to tell because the phases have not necessarily been linear or followed a chronological order. We have been on a spiral, and revisited and reentered phases along the way.

The most persistent and persuasive challenge has been to shift our vision to see what the children are really doing in the classroom every day, to see the interactions, to hear their real conversations, to record these explorations, and to share them with parents, children, and coworkers. A challenge, among many, that Amelia Gambetti passed to us was, "There are elephants walking across your classroom every day and you are focusing on the ants."

To follow Amelia's metaphor, the butterfly has become for us a powerful symbol of self-transformation to represent the stages of our growth. The butterfly is delicate, vulnerable, complicated, evolutionary, cyclical, mystical, and magical and contains within it the genetic components for continual transformation.

The Butterfly Adventure

The Butterfly Adventure

Sandy Burwell and Audrey Favorito

We share with you here images and words from an experience of four-year-old girls and their teachers at the MacDonald Montessori School.

During the time that St. Paul was preparing to host The Hundred Languages of Children exhibit, four children were exploring butterfly stories. There seemed to be a connection between our journey and the stories that the children were creating. The stories evolved into visual expressions, a collaborative book, and an animated video. We then made a public service announcement to share the coming of the exhibit. The children created all the elements and we, as adult collaborators, just offered support of materials, editing, and production.

After the girls viewed the completed thirty-second spot of the public service announcement, the adults thought the project was finished. But the children asked, "Now can we make the long movie?" They were so interested and motivated so we continued creating and filming. In recording notes of our observations, we made the following reflections:

The children have advanced storytelling skills. Collectively the team has a protagonist (butterfly), an antagonist (woodchuck), and a conflict—the essential ingredients to a story.

Their use of fantasy appears to be unbridled.

We've found it's helpful to create the artwork before and during the storytelling sessions. When they have their drawings in front of them, it's easier for them to tell their stories.

The children sometimes collaborate in unison and sometimes break away as individuals, taking ownership of their own twists to the plot. It didn't seem to bother them that the many different experiences of storytelling created many different versions of the story.

In the creative process, the children's relationships and friendships with each other seem to be at the forefront.

They said because they're friends, they want to be together and this project happily accommodated that.

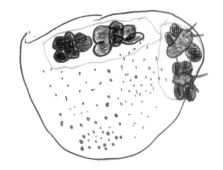

A butterfly was flying in a garden with flowers. Another garden had butterflies and another house had a different garden. In all the gardens, there were magical butterflies and butterflies that weren't magical. The butterflies fly around the garden looking for nectar. They run out of nectar in their home gardens, so they fly all over the country to all the gardens to find nectar. They need to sit down to drink the nectar. They sit down on their legs without bending their knees, because they don't have feet.

There was a woodchuck in one of the gardens. This is the woodchuck. He has a long pointy nose and a sharp pointy back and pink ears. The rest is brown. The woodchuck tried to get the butterflies. The magical butterflies warn the butterflies that were not magical, and they go into the big house so the woodchuck couldn't get them.

All the butterflies got tired. They didn't like the woodchuck because he likes to sneak up on them in the night. They made one big flowerbed so they could all fit in the same bed. They put flowers together. They ripped the petals off and stuck them all together. Then they could sleep with each other 'cause they were all scared. That's why they stay by each other and huddle up.

The butterflies follow a trail and get to where they are supposed to be. They need to sit down to drink nectar on the way. There are butterfly footprints, but they make them with their wings because they don't have feet. This is the map that shows where the butterflies go. The end is where all the footprints go.

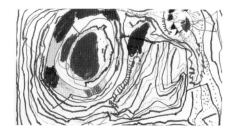

They flew all a long way. They ended up on a really grassy valley. It started to rain a few minutes after they got there and it was purple rain drops. They decided they would live there, and they lived in that place they found ever after. The End

Their Greatest Gift, Our Biggest Challenge

Margie Carter and Deb Curtis

A young teacher in one of our seminars once cautiously raised her hand and asked, "Are you talking about a way of teaching, or a way of living your life?" We had been sharing stories of teachers transcending the limitations and regulations constraining their learning environments. These teachers discovered their new environments provoked more meaningful experiences for the children. They began to see themselves, children, families, and their work as more significant. So we asked this young woman and our seminar group how they would answer the question she posed.

From Reggio we've learned that when you think in terms of values rather than compliance checklists, you open up a new set of possibilities for your school and, indeed, your life. Witness a line in the documentation display at the Chicago Commons Nia Family Center, where a member

The children help carry branches fallen from a tree in a wind storm and work with their families to create a tree house in their classrooms. They become hopeful stewards of the natural world.

of the community said that their new building was a beacon of hope for the neighborhood. The Commons director at the time, Karen Haigh, was fond of quoting the poet Maya Angelou who said, "Every person needs a place that is furnished with hope." This notion is as important to us as the famous quote hanging in the Diana School in Reggio: "Nothing without joy."

The greatest gift and the biggest challenge Reggio educators have brought us is the palpable sense of hope that pierces through our U.S. context with its drive to standardize, commercialize, and quantify the experience of caring for and educating young children. It is not only the beautiful environments, in-depth investigations, and pedagogical documentation which speak to our deepest longings, but the values, relationships, and political intent that underpin these expressions of hope. We are challenged to live with joy and determination even as our country wages war and defines education as getting children ready for economic function, and reduces teaching to scripted curriculum and test scores.

We live in such difficult times with so many factors conspiring to take our dreams away. Yet when Loris Malaguzzi describes the early years of their efforts to recreate schools out of the disasters of fascism and war in their region of Italy, we are humbled. "Finding support for the schools in a devastated town, rich only in mourning and poverty, would be a long and difficult ordeal, and would require sacrifices and solidarity now unthinkable...Some

Intriguing materials call upon the child's imagination and help the child become a creator rather than a consumer.

of the schools would not survive. Most of them, however, would display enough rage and strength to survive."[6] The Reggio experience challenges us to mobilize our resolve and display enough rage, to dare to believe that we, too, can become makers of history.

Ten years ago Deb Curtis left her college teaching job to return to work directly with children, wanting to try to furnish her school with hope. What does this look like? She recently had this dialogue with a visiting delegation of teachers and directors.

The outdoor environment offers a variety of ways to experiment, feel powerful, and find connections to something larger than oneself.

DEB CURTIS: I'm so curious to hear how you are responding to our school because I know it is quite different from yours.

TEACHER 1: I find myself emotional here. This place feels like my home. Where I grew up in Mexico we were free to play outside and relate to nature. What you have here doesn't cost much money but has so much thought and love. Like we did without many resources, you use your imagination with what you have. I can see the children here are critical thinkers. They question things. They know they are competent and you believe in them, so they take risks to explore their big goals. I am emotional because I want this for our children whose families struggled to get to this country with these dreams for their children.

DEB CURTIS: Yes, those are our values in this school. Our goal is for children to self-initiate, question, investigate, and invent. We want them to collaborate, but our emphasis is on negotiating their individual ideas. I've been provoked to examine this more closely after visiting your center. Your children have such a strong group identity that brings obvious joy and a sense of belonging. They were clearly proud to be welcoming visitors and making us feel comfortable, along with encouraging each other. That's not always true in our groups. Our children's collaborative efforts are usually bumpy struggles.

TEACHER 2: Yes. We want our children to have a strong cultural identity as they negotiate the challenges of being new immigrants, learning a new language, and continuing to develop their mother tongue. We need to keep our children safe and ensure they will make it successfully through their schools. I saw your children being critical thinkers and risk takers, and our children need that too in our fight for justice. We have to do both, keep them safe and learning the way the schools expect, but also thinking critically and learning to challenge.

DEB CURTIS: Our children can benefit from a stronger sense of community and seeing themselves as contributing to the larger world rather than primarily acting to meet their individual needs. We must help them develop a growing understanding of how to use their privilege in the world on behalf of working for justice and expanding our democratic ideals. We have to do both too.

This dialogue exemplifies other important challenges from Reggio. We must deeply listen to gather perspectives other than our own, especially those of children. We must learn to welcome and wrestle with different perspectives in our adult conversations, not fear differences or dichotomize them. When we do, something new is born. This will help us create environments of hope.

Reggio educators have inspired us to pursue hope at a larger community and political level, even as we tend to the small details of relationships among people in the school environment. Our deepest hope is that a pedagogy of listening in schools will translate to a pedagogy of diplomacy in the world.

Hope comes from spending a childhood surrounded with familiarity, softness, and materials to discover the possibilities in the world.

School Born as an Art Workshop

Simonetta Cittadini-Medina

Dear Amelia,

When I sit at the plaza and I look at our identity wall, I find evidence of so much of us working and thinking together. There is the timeline, which starts in 1995 and tells the story of our school, recalling the many steps we have taken in our history. The timeline takes me through time, prompting me to travel back and forth. It is a trip with many stops, and I find you in many of them. Do you know that you were part of L'Atelier School even before you visited it in 2000?

I had the vision and the great desire to develop the art workshop into a formal preschool where children and families could find an intelligent space full of provocations to evoke feelings and thinking. You visited our school at the beginning of the millennium. We were thirsty for Reggio ideas and sought your wisdom. You provoked us with the biggest question that can be asked: Who are you?

You touched our souls and invited us to think beyond our daily tasks to become aware of the many whys that form our identity. With you we came closer to ourselves and to our dream: We made our vision a tangible goal. You supported us in finding identity and awareness as our essential anchor, and with it we understood our reasons for our past and our vision for the future. Every visit you paid us brought the important value of creating a dialogue among people. With you we embraced the idea that competition must be replaced with collaboration.

I often think about your role with great admiration. You enter a school as a stranger and find the way to carefully approach the different levels of the school, even sometimes crossing the different boundaries that exist. You do not break any important pillars of the school; instead, you build upon them, making you one more member of the group. You taught us about our own multiculturalism by becoming a little Miamian yourself. You felt the desire to learn to speak Spanish and to become multilingual! You entered our school and opened our eyes to new and innovative ways of teaching. For all this and more, you have become one of us, my dear friend.

Simonetta

Interviews with Three Teachers

Isabel Coles, Claudia Chaustre, and Ana Pineda

I asked three teachers, *"Which aspects have helped you understand the aspect of quality in your work and in the child's work?"*

ISABEL COLES: I think that one of the most important, difficult, and rewarding parts of my process in encountering this approach in the last four years has been my search for quality:

· The quality within myself as an educator not wanting to settle for less, needing to research about different aspects with children.

· Quality within the work with my colleagues. One aspect can be seen in the documentation process we both do. Quality in terms of respecting my own and my colleagues' potential as thinkers who want to act fully, and also as a challenge to continuously provoke ourselves to analyze the child.

· The quality within the child. It starts when the teacher becomes a partner with the child in order to support and provoke the attitude of thinking.

Claudia Chaustre: I consider quality as a chain of aspects that must connect one to the other.

As a teacher, it is essential to make connections between professional development (theory) and my own context in the class and my own personality.

Quality is organization in my work: formulating questions and possible answers, investing time with children in that study. Slowing down means not staying on the surface.

The more you believe in the child, the more you can provoke them. I believe that quality is a constant questioning and rethinking of my work and how I approach it.

**Memory—a collaborative painting
created by children from L'Atelier School.**

ANA PINEDA: The first thing that comes to my mind when I think about quality is the necessity to acquire the attitude of not settling for less and, instead, to strive for a better future for everyone.

Quality makes you think and revisit yourself. Quality comes from my understanding that I need to be open to constructive ideas from others.

When the school and the teachers make the choice to welcome the child with his or her family, a sense of collaboration and exchange is launched. This awakens a dialogue that needs to become an attitude of living, of learning for a common search for quality.

Section Three

Children, Thought, and Learning Made Visible through Documentation

Giovanni Piazza and Sandra Piccinini at
La Villetta School, Reggio Emilia. In the
background is one of the documentation panels
of The Amusement Park for Birds Project.

Contributors

Lilian G. Katz describes the power of an everyday experience: five-year-old children come to know a large supermarket that is next door to their school. They pose questions to the people in the market, and they represent their understandings in multiple ways.

George Forman discusses children's active knowledge construction within a social context, through their immersion in an experience entitled "The Amusement Park for Birds." He analyzes how children express their theories, challenge and support each other's thinking, and reflect on and revise their developing understandings.

Mara Krechevsky writes about the importance of adults asking the right questions, to invite children to articulate their hypotheses and theories, which, in turn, leads children to further investigation and problem-solving. In this case, it is Mara's little boy.

Pam Oken-Wright's poem highlights how a shift of the teacher's view can help the teacher see the child in novel ways. Pam also tells us two stories of how children's exploration and developing understandings are supported by their peers.

Sonya Shoptaugh reminds us about listening to what children have to say in order to know childhood more fully and open the doors for inquiry.

Lynn White narrates about the discovery of the process of understanding documentation as a cooperative endeavor supported and highlighted by colleagues.

Ann Pelo documents how young children make meaning of issues of identity, racial and class differences, and social justice.

Eva Tarini describes an experience in which she documents the work of a child. Eva shares her notebook pages, where she follows and records both the child's narrative and brushstrokes, thereby uncovering an understanding of the child's creative thinking.

Brenda Fyfe gives tribute to Carlina Rinaldi, who inspires a group of college students to question their certainties, think from multiple perspectives, give value to difference, and, above all, listen carefully.

"Teachers must leave behind an isolated, silent mode of working, which leaves no traces. Instead they must discover ways to communicate and document the children's evolving experiences at school. They must prepare a steady flow of quality information targeted to parents but appreciated by children and teacher." [1]

LORIS MALAGUZZI

"Documentation (like observation) involves questions of value. It offers a true experience of democracy because democracy also means exchange, and this exchange is made possible by the visibility and the recognition of differences and subjectivity. When differences and subjectivities are in dialogue, they become educational values that are not only declared but also lived.

"Documentation, or all the materials produced during observation, is also an important instrument for the children. Through procedures that are analogous to those of the adults, children can see themselves in a new light, and revisit and reinterpret their own experiences of the events in which they were direct protagonists. This kind of process produces new cognitive dynamics, a new and different vision of oneself and one's action in relation to others, and this is true for children as well as adults. To experience a process and see it reproduced (that is, see ourselves reproduced) in the documentation—and thus in the thought—of another person, creates the sort of disorientation that opens the way to amazement, doubt, and desire to know more and to know ourselves better." [2]

CARLINA RINALDI

A Celebration

Lilian G. Katz

There are so many aspects of the Reggio Emilia experience to celebrate that it is hard to know where to begin. The Reggio approach to the care and education of young children has captured the attention and appreciation of early childhood educators around the world. In just a few decades their work has had worldwide impact on how we understand the best ways to nurture our youngest children.

As I reflect on the sixteen years since the first of my thirteen visits to Reggio Emilia, I must put high on my list of many things for which I am grateful to our Reggio colleagues both the insights and the inspiration they have provided.

In terms of insights, too numerous to outline here, I often turn to one of many favorite examples of the quality of the children's work captured in a book titled *Noi i bimbi e lui Gulliver* (We Children and He Gulliver), published by the municipality of Reggio Emilia in 1984. This little book documents a study, made by some four- and five-year-olds, of the huge supermarket next door to their school. The documentation of their experiences offers rich insights into the multiple ways that young children can represent what they see, what they notice, what they observe, and what they find out about the complex activities, events, objects, and materials around them.

This large drawing of the Co-op Supermarket was created by two of the children involved in the investigation who combined the representations of many of their classmates into the one comprehensive picture shown here. Encouraging young children to make such creative use of their peers' work was totally new to me, and served as a source of insight into how adults can help children build a community of scholars, even in the early years.

A major inspiration emerging from multiple experiences with Reggio colleagues and their practices is that the careful documentation of children's experiences can speak for themselves. Indeed, the extensive and beautiful documentation of the children's experiences has caused the entire international early childhood education community to strive to develop more appropriate, effective, and beneficial experiences for the world's young children than has ever been offered before. The exquisite documentation of the profoundly engaging experiences provided to young children in the city of Reggio Emilia confirms the truism that what we do speaks more loudly than what we say.

Noi i bimbi e lui Gulliver

Book cover published by municipality of Reggio Emilia, 1984, Preschool Ada Gobetti.

We Children and He Gulliver (Noi i bimbi e lui Gulliver)[3]
An Excerpt from the Story

Municipality of Reggio Emelia

In the neighborhood of the Ada Gobetti Preschool, a large supermarket opened a few years before this experience with the children and teachers. Every year about 65,000 children enter this cooperative supermarket. It is a phenomenon that teachers felt could not be ignored, and should invite reflection and inquiry among teachers and with children. Who are the children and what age are they expected or required to accompany the parents to do this chore? What kind of image do the children have of themselves and of the supermarket environment while the parents are involved in their shopping task? What questions do the children have? What do they enjoy? What attracts their attention?

There are many possible ways to take stock of this complex cultural phenomenon that has been developing in a small city that used to have many small stores and still has an open air market twice a week. The teachers pose a question to the children: "Why do people go to the cooperative supermarket?"

One of the answers: "If there is no more food at home, the people cannot stay without food for a long time because they would die. So they go to the cooperative and they buy everything—food, clothing, toys, and also chewing gum."

One day the teachers obtain the permission to visit the cooperative supermarket before it opens. The empty space that they enter, without the many people, invites the children to make many observations:

You might get lost here more than in a street.

It is like inside the whale of Pinocchio.

It is large like a forest, maybe like a bear.

It seems like a room…for swimming.

There is a million carts.

The people of the Co-op divide things in half, one thing on a shelf, another thing on another.

Another day the teacher asks a group of children to compile a shopping list and then, as if in a treasure hunt, accompanies them to the supermarket where the children experience finding the things from the list on the shelves. They then meet all together at the cash register with the teacher. What do they do next?

Put all what we got on that thing that moves toward the cashier.

She looks at the things to sell and if the things are good she puts a high price.

She presses a button and the price comes out in a ticket.

You give her the money.

She gives you some change.

She will take a bag and put everything in the bag. Sometimes you need many bags.

The relationship with the cashier is a bit of a mystery. What does the cashier do with all the money she gets? Teachers reflect. How do children find out the way a supermarket works and the different roles of the people who work there? What kind of words do the adults, who are not usually in contact with children, use to explain their work?

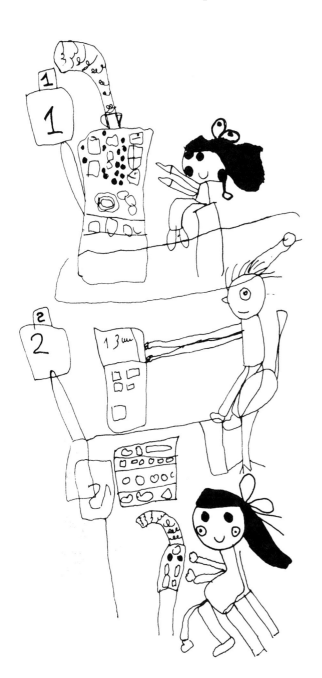

The teachers decide with the children: Let us ask the cashier.

CHILD: Who keeps the money that the people give you?

CASHIER: The cashier cannot keep the money and take it home, otherwise she would be rich. She gives the money to the manager, who takes it to the bank.

CHILD: Why to the bank?

CASHIER: He takes the money to the bank because we have to pay for all the merchandise that we buy in order to sell it to the people.

CHILD: How can you remember the price of everything?

CASHIER: Because the price is written on each thing. Everything has a price written. I read it and then I write on the machine.

CHILD: How come that is the price that comes into the machine?

CASHIER: There are liquid crystals like a quartz watch. It works in the same way.

CHILD: Your machine works with a battery or with a light bulb?

CASHIER: It works with electricity, like a light bulb.[3]

It Can Be Done and Also Revised

George Forman

Good teaching needs to be demonstrated for others to learn and to value its form. We in North America are grateful for the care with which the educators in Reggio Emilia have documented constructivist education. I am most familiar with their work via the three years that Lella Gandini and I, with the leadership of Loris Malaguzzi, Amelia Gambetti, Carlina Rinaldi, and Giovanni Piazza, created the documentary video *The Amusement Park for Birds*. Through this project I saw many principles of constructivist education placed into an integrated way of working, in this case, at La Villetta School in Reggio Emilia.

How often we hear principles of education, but have no living examples. At La Villetta, the principles of social constructivism unfolded as we filmed. Filippo designed a water wheel using five

different media, got criticism from his friends, contradictions from the different media and, in the end, figured out the difference between the ornamental and the functional parts of his water wheel. Georgia and Simone debated the difference between the total number of clay sprays Georgia's fountain needed versus the number of clay sprays remaining to be placed. Andrea drew the entire underground system of water pipes, but then had to explain to his friends why he had omitted the water itself.

Filippo draws a water wheel that has trapped a bird, causing him to think about the paddle as something that scoops things up.

Using social constructivism as a framework, the teachers in Reggio offer children the representational tools, the space, the time, and the confidence to challenge and support each other's thinking. The teachers realize that true knowledge consists of the child's ability to communicate reasons for action, not simply lists of facts.

These actions range from drawing marks to communicating an idea to playing a game that is explained by the rationale of its rules. In moments throughout the day, children are encouraged to express, reflect, explain, and revise—all in a social context of communication, trust, and continuity across time and friendship.

Filippo blows on the windmill to see how a steady force in one direction can make an object spin around.

Filippo tests open copper loops on his water wheel, perhaps thinking about his drawing of the trapped bird. Georgia says these loops are playing tricks with the water. Filippo adds solid paddles.

"Why Don't You Tell the Other Kids?"

*Mara Krechevsky**

One late March day not long ago, I was walking to preschool with my four-year-old son, Caleb, when he turned to me and asked, "How do leaves get back on trees?" I responded, "What do you think?"

CALEB: I don't know. *Silence*

ME: Do you have any ideas?

CALEB: Maybe people come around and find them on the ground and pick them up and put them back on the trees.

ME: That's an interesting theory. Do you know what a theory is?

CALEB: No.

ME: It's an idea you have about how to make sense of things you don't understand. *Silence* Why don't you tell the other kids in your class your theory and see what they think. *Silence*

ME: Have you ever seen anyone do this?

CALEB: No.

ME: So that's more information for your theory. *Silence*

CALEB: I don't think kids could do it because they're not big enough…well, maybe some teenagers could.

*With many thanks to teacher Ellen Goldberg for her careful and sensitive listening and priceless documentation.

"Annaliese is dusting Slater," says Annaliese

"Slater looks like he is in a leaf storm."
—Annaliese

We arrived at Caleb's classroom and I mentioned our conversation to his teacher, Ellen, who asked Caleb to share his theory with the class. After hearing Caleb's ideas, his classmate Camila pointed out that even grownups couldn't reach the high branches on trees. Someone probably used a cherry-picker truck to put the leaves back on the branches. Taigue suggested that leaves grow from buds, and Philip said buds grow from inside the branch. The children suggested an experiment: get branches, put dirt on them, then put leaf seeds on them and see if buds grow.

They collected branches on the playground, but the next day Ellen said she had looked everywhere, but couldn't find any leaf seeds. The children looked at the branches and a new question came up: "If the branch is broken from the tree, can it still grow?" A new experiment began. Branches were placed in different situations. To determine whether the branches were growing, the children decided to measure them with plastic links. Jake suggested taking a photograph of the branch with buds to remember what it looked like at the beginning of the experiment.

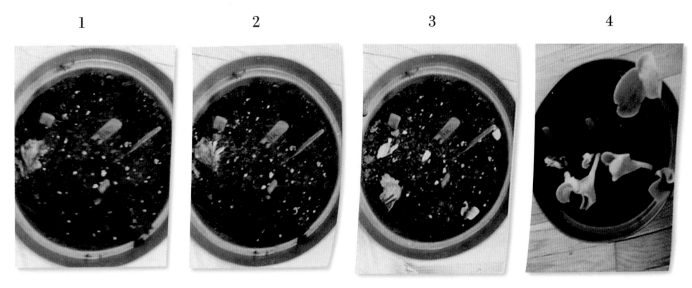

1   2   3   4

What is in these pictures? Can you see what is different in each picture?

The branch with the buds grew while the others did not. Though the buds opened, no leaves came out. "Strings with little green flowers at the end" grew instead. Then the "strings" died and little green leaves started to grow. After the experiment, Ellen asked the children what they had learned so far. Caleb said, "I learned that leaves come from buds. They grow from inside the branch, but I don't know how. I also learned that if you put a branch from the ground in water, it won't grow. Taking pictures is good so you can see how the buds change."

Since my encounter with Reggio, I have changed the way I interact with children. I don't accept an initial "I don't know." I allow for silence. I wait more. I encourage children to share their ideas with other children, and refer them to other children to find things out. I try to understand and explore their worldview for longer time, rather than lead

them (even if ever so gently) to another one. I value whimsy and fantasy, along with science, in the development of their theories. I am more comfortable with conflicting thoughts and ideas, and consider us all intellectuals learning from and with one another. And I am a better listener, but will always need to work on improving that quality.

Later that same day, Caleb and I were walking to the park and he noticed some buds on the trees. "Mom—look at that, I see buds." I answer, "That's great. More information. Why don't you tell the other kids?"

"Dillon is picking up the leaves." says Annaliese.

Rare Visions

Pam Oken-Wright

*I have come to understand that the world
is only as ordinary as I choose it to be.
It's a choice between taking the world for
granted, assuming I know enough about
a thing, and engaging the rare vision
that comes from "seeing again."*

A shift of the lens
makes the image new,
the teacher's image nudged by
observing and documenting,
the child's image
by representing what she sees and knows
 and imagines,
through and for the sake of relationship
with others
with ideas
with the world.

A shift of the teacher's lens
toward children's relationships and
 representation,
bending light toward what the children
 have to say,
suddenly makes visible
intellectual electricity
and joy of a discovery shared.

A shift of the lens
suddenly makes visible
the way a child's image of herself transforms,
in turn marking changes in the relationship
between the child and the world.

A shift of the lens
suddenly makes visible
the slow, sure growth of a culture
that will belong only and ever to the children
who create it.

A shift of the lens
suddenly makes visible
that which must have always been there
for the looking,
a realm of possibilities
and a glimpse at the face of brilliance
a thousand times a day.

In the first days of school, five-year-old Caroline spent quite a bit of time with Peep, one of our three pet finches. On this day Caroline set out to draw a portrait of Peep. As she drew, she spoke of her hope that Peep would see the portrait and be her friend; this picture was intended to feed the relationship Caroline felt growing between them.

When she finished drawing Peep, she rose from the table, thought again, and returned to write the bird's name and hers. When she was satisfied, she approached the cage and held the picture up for Peep to see, her expression one of anticipation. "Do you think he likes it?" she wondered aloud.

Isabel Makes her Idea Visible with the Support of the Group

On this day in early January, a small group of children chooses to work with clay in the studio. As soon as they sit down, they begin to discuss their plans. "I'm going to make a horse," says one. "Me, too," decides another and another. "Let's make one big horse," someone suggests. They all think that this is a good idea, but as they discuss the possibility the plan evolves. They decide, instead, to make a horse family, and then assign themselves particular members of the horse family to make. I am intrigued by the children's apparent expectation of collaboration—such a big part of all they are doing at this time of year—even in a medium that so easily lends itself to individual endeavor.

Isabel decides to make the "lying down one" in the horse family. This was a concept more difficult to execute than to imagine. With a picture of a reclining horse to use as a referent and the support of her classmates and teacher, Isabel is able to make a "lying down horse" that pleases her, and impresses everyone else.

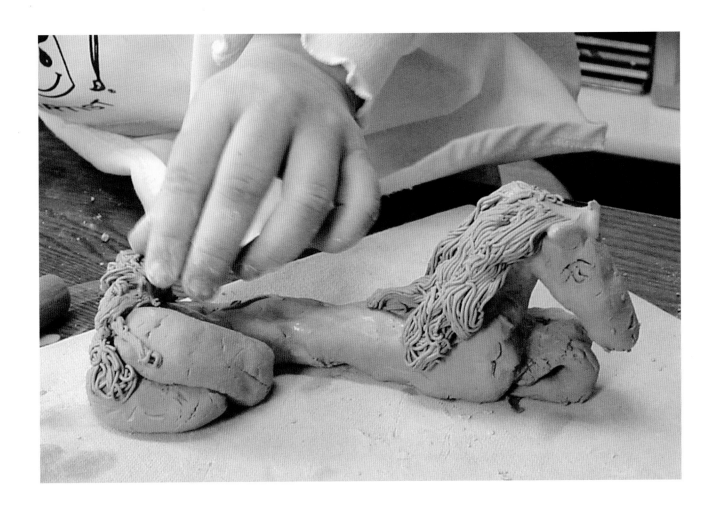

In the autumn, a sycamore tree in our outdoor play space yields huge leaves that spark the children's awe and imagination. Here the children use contour drawing techniques—following the edge of the leaf with the eye (and sometimes with the finger) while letting the other hand follow the same path with pencil or with paint. Arlo completes the outline of the leaf in this way and is now adding the veins that she sees. In the background, Elizabeth just begins the process with a smaller leaf.

Listen to the Children

Sonya Shoptaugh

Children have thoughts. They have opinions. They have interests. They have unique perspectives about how the world works. This may seem obvious, and as a young teacher right out of college, I would have agreed with all those statements—in theory. In action, I went about my school days doing a lot of talking and very little listening to children. I didn't realize this until Amelia Gambetti, a teacher from Reggio Emilia, began to work with us at the Model Early Learning Center in Washington, DC.

During one of our first marathon staff meetings, we moaned to Amelia about how we couldn't do projects because our children weren't interested in anything and, besides, we didn't have any stone lions near our school. We had seen the film, *A Portrait of a Lion*, where she and her children were involved in a magnificent project about the lion statues in their Italian town square. We were inspired and depressed at the same time. If only we had a piazza and some stone lions, then we could do a project. After hearing our rather pathetic

excuses, I'm amazed Amelia didn't pack her bags and return to Italy that day! Instead, she said with force, "Look outside your window! What do you see?" I begged my brain to come up with something because I could tell Amelia meant business. One of the teachers tentatively said, "The Capitol." "Right!" Amelia boomed. "The Capitol! A project about the Capitol! Yes! And you have an elephant walking through your school, and all you see are ants!"

Ants, ants, my mind was racing...I couldn't recall any ants. At that moment, Coco, our school cat, helped me out by rubbing up against my legs. Oh, yes, our resident elephant, who could offer us so many possibilities, if only we would recognize what we had in front of us.

Once we opened our eyes, we began to see how Coco was a very special character in our school. He played an important role in our daily lives and in developing the personality of our school.

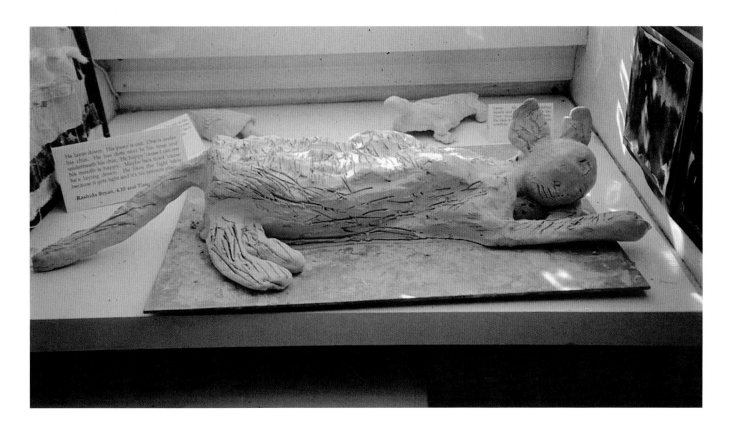

Coco also helped us, as teachers, learn how to listen more closely to children. We noticed how the children loved to follow him around, play with him, find his hiding places, pet and hold him. They respected his needs, desires, and rights—they valued his presence in the school.

At a subsequent staff meeting, we continued to discuss project development and the importance of knowing children and their points of view. Amelia casually mentioned, "You could have a conversation with children about Coco." I wasn't sure what she meant. It sounded revolutionary. "You mean, sit down and just talk with them?"

Amelia nodded and said, "Yes, you sit down and talk with them, and you listen and you hear what they have to say." Wow, I thought. How come I never thought of doing that before?

Through Amelia's masterful guidance and the inspiration we received from the infant/toddler centers and preschools of Reggio Emilia, we discovered children, our children, and the power of relationships cultivated through listening. We learned to value the richness of our own context. By knowing our children more fully, we could support higher quality experiences in connection with their unique lives and experience the joy that comes from vibrant learning.

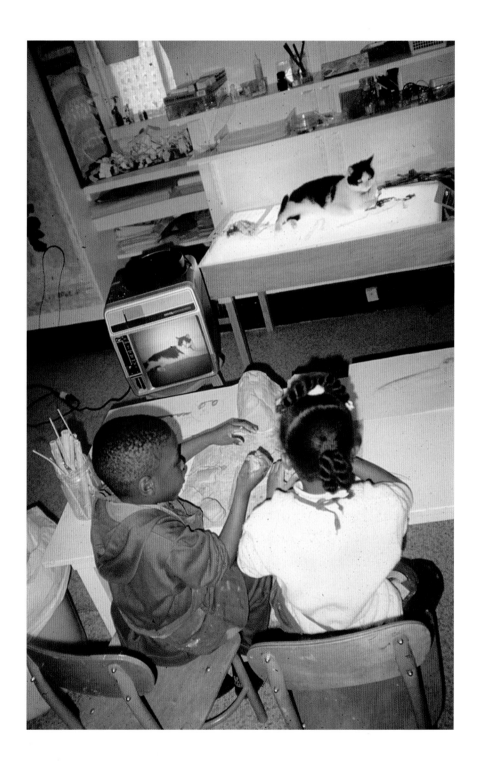

ANTONIO: Coco loves to play with us.

TERRELL: He has friends at school.

KRISTEN: The children are his friends.

ARMINTA: Coco is smart.

IBRAHIM: I like Coco very much.

ANTWAN: I like the way he eats his food.

IBRAHIM: Is Coco fat? I think he's fat because he eats a lot!

DIARA: He eats cake.

ANTWAN: No, he don't. He eats cat food cereal.

IBRAHIM: I can pet Coco because he likes me.

ABDULAH: When we aren't here, Amelia takes care of Coco.

Interpreting Experiences and Creating Documentation of Children's Environments

Lynn White

Since my first visit to Reggio Emilia in June of 1991, our school district has had ongoing experiences and relationships with the educators from Reggio. We continue to be involved with the work of Reggio and feel fortunate to participate in whatever opportunities arise for us. On one occasion a number of years ago, we heard from our director of professional development, Mary Mumbrue, that Lella Gandini would be visiting us and that she would spend two half days in each of the three elementary buildings. Based on our needs and desires at the time, we could design whatever experience we wanted to further our thinking around ideas from Reggio. We didn't know then that we would be creating an experience that would be pivotal for us in furthering our understanding of collaboration and the role of documentation.

The Learning Experience

Lella arrived at Greeley School for our time together. Four K-2 teachers joined Lella, and together we drove to a school board member's house to have lunch and begin our work. We had been grappling with the idea of creating documentation panels but had felt sort of "stuck" in our work. The panels we had created up until that point were usually constructed by individual teachers with or without their students, but today, I was to present a classroom experience to this group (6–7 of us in total) and work to uncover this "mystery" of creating documentation panels together. The experience that I shared was about children creating personal spaces in the loft that they had designed and a parent had built for us earlier that year. I was overwhelmed when trying to think about how to take this in-depth experience and condense it into two panels of documentation. As I was gathering all of the documentation to bring to this meeting, I reviewed again, as I often do, words from a Reggio educator. In this case it was Amelia Gambetti, and her words were about why we revisit documentation. As I read over her words, I saw once again the importance of this step in our daily work with children and in our collaborations with others: "We revisit to observe again, recognize yourself, remember, find new ways of describing something, and make predictions about next steps."

Lella asked me to begin by telling the story about the loft. She asked the rest of the group to take notes on what they heard and also to jot down what they noticed or wondered about. They then shared their notes and their own observations with the group and I took notes. After that sharing (which was more thoughtful and thorough than I could have imagined), I shared what I was hoping to communicate through the panels. As a group, we put all of these observations and interpretations together with my hopes for communication, and decided what the main points were and how we might design these panels. Each person drew her or his design and, after sharing these individual plans with the group, we made our final design together. At this point, I was asked by the group to go back

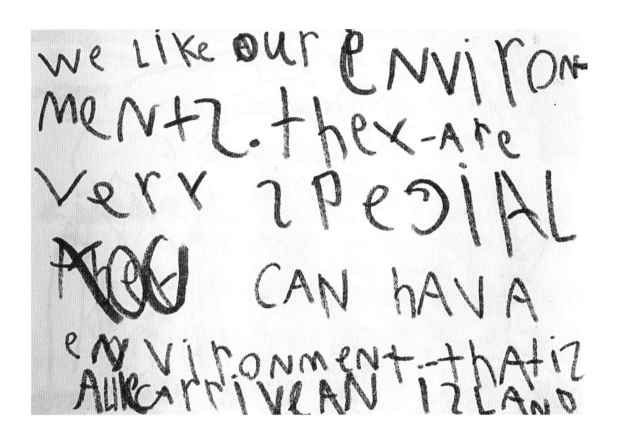

we like our environ-mentz. they-are very zpeoial you can hava environment that iz alikarrivean izland

to the students to collect their drawings and words about how the pulley works in the loft and to find and enlarge some photos of the loft as it was being constructed.

Lella then shared some important aspects of "reading panels" in process and suggested:

choosing a title from the words of children, followed by a quote from (me) the classroom teacher

remembering that we "read panels" from left to right, top to bottom

enlarging some of the photos, photocopying some of the children's drawings (if necessary shrinking them), and placing them to emphasize a certain part of the experience

placing the photos, captions, and transcriptions of children's words in a way to read them easily

communicating to the reader of the panels my intent and our (the group's) interpretation of the children's work, and of their ideas and hypotheses as well.

After we decided on the final design of the two panels, we then listed the documentation that had to be gathered or the work that had to be done before we met again, and to my surprise, everyone volunteered to help in this work. We decided as a group on the next provocation to offer to my students in this process and created another meeting time to revisit the children's ideas and drawings from this new provocation. What a joy it was to feel that everyone joined to help with the work and interpretation! In the meantime, we met again with Lella a few days later and, as a group, completed our collaborative work in creating these two documentation panels.

Reflection

After Lella left, our group met to reflect on this experience together. We felt we had learned so much from Lella and each other, and that helped us to further our understanding in many ways.

We recognized and valued our district's support of our learning. By giving us two afternoons out of the classroom and by allowing us to have support to design our experience based on our needs and desires at the time, we noted the following:

One recent fall, the children and I had a conversation about environments to express our different viewpoints and to come to an understanding of what we think an environment is. We then closed our eyes to get an image of an environment that is/was special to us in our lives. The following drawings and words represent our thinking.

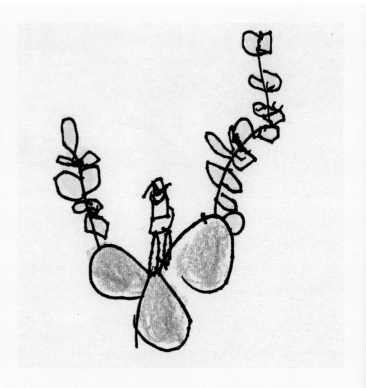

STANLEY: My special environment is a tree. I'm sitting on a tree.

LYNN: What makes this environment so important?

STANLEY: I like sitting in a tree.

- We appreciated the support of the school board member in knowing about Reggio, in her desire to join in the learning, and by offering her home as an informal environment without interruptions.

- We saw firsthand the power of multiple perspectives in listening, sharing, and interpreting children's work.

- We remembered the important role that relationship plays in our work with children and each other.

- We learned so much about the design of documentation panels.

- We realized that my observation of the thoughtfulness and thoroughness of the group in their observations and notes directly mirrored our observations of children when they work and think in these ways.

- We all felt very thankful that we were given the time to be together to uncover and interpret this experience, and to create documentation panels.

ERIC: My special environment is in the state capitol in Springfield, and I'm looking up and I can see lots of colors.

LYNN: What makes this environment so special?

ERIC: Because it looks so neat.

AMANDA: My special environment is on the roller coaster and it's called The Whizzer. This is me and this is a giant flower.

LYNN: what makes this environment special?

AMANDA: It has a lot of turns that you go sideways on.

We all noticed and valued the respect and regard we felt for children's work and ideas, and teachers' work and ideas. Years later, we all remember so much about those two afternoons together. As Lella reminded us, "Revisiting helps children, as well as teachers, to become aware of children's learning and then also to learn how to learn." Nothing is more powerful.

CARLY K.: My special environment is a swing set at my house. One of my favorite things to do—I have two—are the swings and the rings.

LYNN: What makes this environment so special?

CARLY K.: I like swinging because it feels like flying, and I like climbing and sitting up there.

HALEY: My special environment is my grandma's house. This is where me and my cousins sleep. This is where my nana and papa sleep and Mom and Dad sleep here. My cousins go down there—there's room behind the kitchen. Aunt Elizabeth goes there. My aunt Dale sleeps right there. The house is in New Hampshire.

LYNN: What makes this environment so important?

HALEY: It makes me think that it's really fun, there's a lot of really fun stuff there.

JACK: My special environment is when I was on a trip skiing with my dad.

LYNN: What makes this environment so special?

JACK: Because it was fun with my dad.

MARTHA: My special environment is I'm climbing a tree in my backyard.

LYNN: What makes this environment so special?

MARTHA: I like trees a lot.

Pedagogical Documentation and Change

Ann Pelo

Too often in our field, passionate advocates of anti-bias practices and committed practitioners of Reggio-inspired pedagogy live in separate worlds, each with its own focus, vocabulary, and teaching emphases and practices. These two arenas are perceived as distinct and self-contained, with little exchange or dialogue between them. But at the crossroads where social justice work and Reggio-inspired teaching meet, we are called to weave together a commitment to responsive pedagogy with a commitment to work for just, nonviolent communities.

The schools in Reggio Emilia were created at the end of World War II as an act of determined, fierce hope—an act of resistance to the fascism that had taken hold of Italy during the 1920s, 1930s, and early 1940s, and a bold commitment to create a new culture. Loris Malaguzzi located the birth of the schools in this political context, saying, "We are part of an ongoing story of men and women, ideals intact, who realize that history can be changed, and that it is changed starting with the future of children."[4]

The commitment to change history gave birth to a pedagogy that demands critical thinking and engaged participation in the life of the community by children, teachers, and families. Reggio-inspired pedagogy is a way of being in the world—a way of seeing, listening, speaking, a commitment to relationships that honor identity and culture, a commitment to dialogue and action. It grows from and returns to listening, with an open and curious heart. When we listen in this way, we hear children's efforts to make meaning of issues of identity, difference, justice, and equity.

When we listen to the children as they pursue questions of identity, culture, and community, they will lead us right to the intersection with social justice issues. And that is the moment of truth for us: will we journey to this intersection with them, affirming our belief that they are resourceful, engaged participants in their communities, able to think critically and act with determined conviction, or will we turn aside, unwilling to take up the challenging, invigorating work of exploring issues related to race, class, body size and ability, family make-up, and gender?

To truly embrace the pedagogy and values of the schools in Reggio Emilia, we must honor their political legacy. We honor this legacy by joining their efforts to create a culture of deep listening, compassionate perspective-taking, critical thinking, and strong action in the face of injustice. We honor this legacy by cultivating what author, naturalist, and environmental activist Terry Williams calls "democracy as a way of life: the right to be educated, to think, discuss, dissent, create, and act, acting in imaginative and revolutionary ways."[5] In this way, we become part of the ongoing story of men and women determined to change history.

We hear three-year-old girls seeking to understand power, gender, and identity:

ANNA: Jessa has a little power. She doesn't have enough, because she's little and so she has only a little power.

RACHEL: Anna, Jessa has control of her own body. You are not the truth of her body. Her body does have power! There's little power and big power right in her belly. It's inside you and you can have enough power. Jessa can have enough power.

TEACHER MOLLY: Tell me more about who has power.

RACHEL: Only the boys and the big girls. My brother is a boy, and he's strong and he has power.

JESSA: When I grow big, I'll have power.

TEACHER MOLLY: How big do you need to grow to have power?

JESSA: A little bit big. I do have power now because I'm a little bit big.

We hear four- and five-year-old European-American children trying to make sense of brown skin in a culture that privileges whiteness:

"Is your skin getting darker while you get older?" a child asks Miriam, a teacher who is Filipino.

"Your hair goes with your skin, and you have brown eyes, too," another child comments to Miriam, stroking her dark hair and her dark skin.

"Brown babies come from brown mamas, right?" a third child asks. "Is your mama brown, Miriam? Did she get brown when she got old to be a mom?"

We hear six- and seven-year-old children exploring issues of class and wealth:

CARL: Most of the kids at John Hay School are richer than us.

OLIVER: Yeah, Drew and Molly get all the toys that they want.

CARL: And you only buy more toys if you have more money.

LUCY: But some kids buy their own toys from their allowance; their parents don't buy the toys.

OLIVER: Yeah, but their parents give them all the money to buy them, so it's the same thing.

To Observe and Document a Meaningful Moment in a Child's Life

Eva Tarini

These images represent an exceptional experience from my year in Reggio Emilia. I was spending time with the four-year-olds at the Diana School. That day I watched while two children painted on opposite sides of an easel. The boy worked silently, but the girl was talking both to herself and to the boy. I soon realized that she was narrating the story in her painting. To merely glance at her work, one would not readily identify the protagonists because the painting was entirely abstract. This fascinated me and I quickly tried to copy her painting into my notebook, while simultaneously recording her words.

Later I worked with Vea and Laura to create a panel that presented the progression of the painting with its accompanying narrative, rendering a rather private moment public, and uncovering the creative thinking of this child.

For me, this brief observation, and the subsequent documentation we created, embodies many elements that were fundamental to my learning: recognizing the extraordinary in an ordinary moment; learning to observe closely and take meaningful notes; working with others to analyze and theorize about children's work; meeting with others to create a piece of documentation that faithfully communicates a moment in a child's life and that emphasizes the thought that children bring to their work; and, much later, creating a slide show and description of this experience to share at workshops.

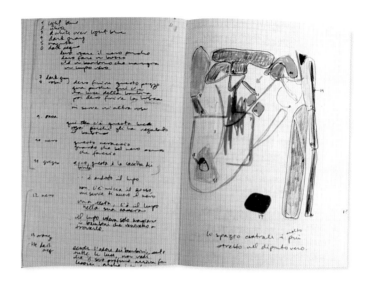

Fourteen years later, this remains a singular memory. It took place during a year that enveloped me in thinking. I observed, discussed, wrote, discussed, thought, discussed, rethought, and absorbed so much about the possibilities and responsibilities of working with children. It changed me as a teacher, and I will carry it with me always.

These are notes I took at that time:

A child paints. A teacher observes; she writes down what the child says, and notes the formal and chromatic evolution of the painting.

While Elisa paints, she speaks out loud, tells a story, creates and develops a story. When she begins, she identifies characters and invents locations, each one a color that becomes a symbol: a wolf is represented by black; two children (a boy and a girl) by two different tones of pink that she defines as "the lights"; the wolf's house is light gray.

Then the story lights up, told with great skill through brushstrokes of color, which, notwithstanding occasional interruptions, are always able to relate to the plot and follow the color symbols that she assigned. The dark blue is utilized to represent both the perfume of the children and the odor of the wolf; the voice of the wolf is red; the pink light, which symbolizes the boy, is so powerfully blinding that it can defeat the wolf.

And thus appear, in a nonfigurative painting, active characters, alive places, strong actions, words, power, and feelings.

All this makes very concrete the importance of listening and observing while children are working and playing. It is not enough to look at the finished painting and to ask, "What did you paint?" and perhaps to even add, "It's beautiful. You did a good job."

Having followed this painting throughout its construction, we are permitted not only to see better, but our understanding of the richness of children's work is heightened.

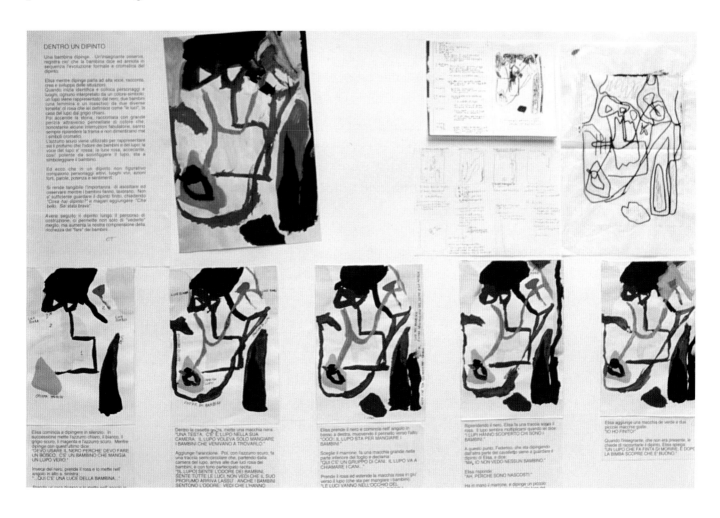

Elisa begins painting in silence. In succession, she uses light blue, white, dark gray, magenta, and dark blue. While she paints with this last color, she says: *I need to use black because I have to make a forest. There is a little boy who is eating a real wolf.*

Instead of black, however, she takes the pink and puts it in the upper left-hand corner: *Here is the light of the little girl.*

She then takes another shade of pink and she puts it in the upper right-hand corner: *Here is the pink light of the little boy.*

Silently, she adds the previously mentioned black, then the light gray, and she says: *There. This is the children's house.*

Inside the gray house, she makes a black mark: *A head. The wolf is in his room. The wolf only wanted to eat the children who came to visit him.*

She adds some orange. Then, with the dark blue, she makes a semicircular track, which, starting from the wolf's room, arrives at the two pink lights of the children, and with a dramatic tone she recites: *The wolf smells the odor of the children, he smells all the lights. Don't you see that his perfume reaches all the way up there? Even the children smell the odor; can you see that they have sniffed him?*

She takes the red, moves the brush from the gray triangle down toward the house and then up toward the light of the little boy, and she says: *Here the wolf is talking to his friends, do you see?*

Elisa takes the black and begins in the lower right-hand corner, moving the brush up toward the top: *OOO...the wolf is about to eat the children.*

She chooses the brown, makes a large mark in the lower part of the paper, and exclaims: *Here is the group of dogs. The wolf is going to call the dogs.*

She takes the pink and extends it down toward the wolf (who is about to eat the children): *The lights are going into the eye of the wolf, then the wolf becomes blind.*

Elisa adds a green mark and then two yellow spots, and she announces: *I am finished.*

When the teacher, who was not present while Elisa was painting, asks her to explain the painting, Elisa explains: *A wolf pretended to die, and afterwards the little girl discovers that he is good.*

Taking the black once again, Elisa makes a mark on top of the pink. The wolf seems to multiply when she says: *The wolves have discovered who the children are.*

At this point, Federico, who has been painting on the other side of the easel, comes around to look at Elisa's painting, and he says: *But I don't see the children.*

Elisa answers: *Ah, that's because they are hiding.*

In her hand she has the brown, and she paints a little triangle to the right, up near the light of the boy. She turns to Federico and says: *I made a piece of a rifle.*

Photograph of Elisa's original painting.

Learning with Carlina Rinaldi

Brenda Fyfe

We came as individuals to a class, with a mutual interest in a subject. We left as group learners, with a mutual interest in each other. We learned to give value to each other's subjectivity and intersubjectivity. Carlina helped us to realize and feel that we exist with others and through others. As she predicted, this helped us to form a new image of the human being and humanity.

> *We learned to listen more closely to children*
> *and each other, to share our observations and*
> *documentation with the group,*
> *and to engage in a collaborative process*
> *of reflection that is critical to group learning.*

In the fall of 2001, Carlina came to Webster University as a visiting professor and co-taught a graduate course on "Observation and Documentation." At a time when our lives and our worlds were shaken by the events of September 11, she helped us to question our certainties, to give value to difference, and to think from multiple perspectives as we explored the power of fear in the lives of children and ourselves. She reminded us, "The relationship between the individual and others, between Self and Other, is a key issue for our futures."

Carlina Rinaldi

Section Four

The Hundred Languages of Children: The Role of Materials and the Atelier

Giovanni Piazza, Vea Vecchi, and Mara Davoli:
Three *atelieristi* selecting slides for a documentary
to be presented for professional development.

Contributors

Jennifer Azzariti describes the power and potential of exploring and using recycled and natural materials with children to express ideas and understandings.

Pauline M. Baker reflects on the importance of creating an aesthetic and intentional space for exploration and learning. She tells a story of how a weaving project invites collaboration and conversation, thereby strengthening a sense of community within this bilingual school in the Southwest.

Karen Haigh tells us about four-year-old Angelica's exploration with language, print, and illustration, further supported and developed by her teacher's questions and sensitive presence.

Pam Houk's poem and story remind us of the importance of preparing experiences and environments that invite and support children's investigations and discoveries.

Shareen Abramson makes a connection between the theory of "the hundred languages" and the theory of semiotics proposed by the northern Italian linguist Umberto Eco. She sees this connection as a means to understand better the learning process of English language learners in developing communicative literacy.

Lynn Hill describes an intergenerational atelier and how it creates empathic relationships among children and older adults.

Patricia Hunter McGrath uses the metaphor of a dance in a poem that expresses how an abundance of expressive materials can create wonder, passion, joy, and connectedness.

"*The atelier was never intended as a sort of secluded, privileged space, as if it were only there that the languages of expressive art could be produced. It was, instead, a place where children's different languages could be explored by them and studied by us in a favorable and peaceful atmosphere.*

We and they could experiment with alternative modalities, techniques, instruments, and materials; explore themes chosen by children or suggested by us; perhaps work on a large fresco in a group; perhaps prepare a poster where one makes a concise statement through words and illustrations; perhaps even master small projects on a reduced scale, stealing the skills from architects! What was important was to help the children find their own styles of exchanging with friends both their talents and their discoveries...

The atelier, a space rich in materials, tools, and people with professional competence, has contributed much to our work on documentation. This work has strongly informed—little by little—our way of being with children...But the atelier was most of all a place for research, and we expect that it will continue to increase."[1]

LORIS MALAGUZZI

Before I Saw Images from Reggio

Jennifer Azzariti

Before Amelia Gambetti came, I relied on what I knew from my own childhood experiences and from what I saw in other schools—traditional early childhood "art," using traditional store-bought materials. I didn't know what else there could be beyond finger painting. I didn't realize the potential and capabilities of young children. Once I saw images from Reggio and began to think about other ways of working, I flourished.

It was a revelation to put the same thinking, organization, and care into working with materials and children that I would into my own work.

It was liberating to think and make choices as opposed to following recipes for art projects, to work and learn alongside children instead of teaching something to them. I appreciated the back-and-forth nature of the relationships with children.

  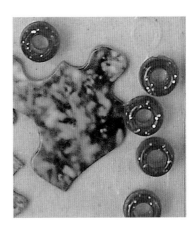

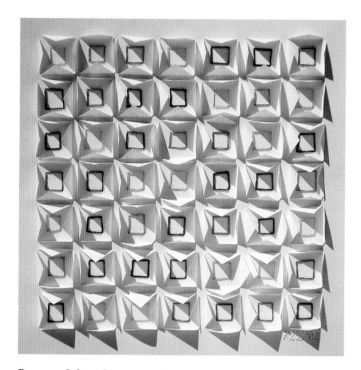

Paper and thread constructions

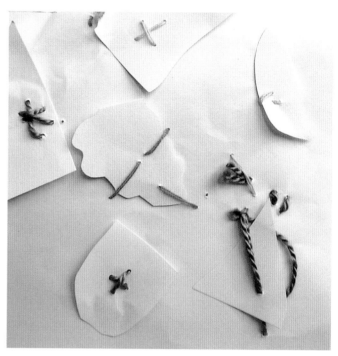

Paper and thread constructions

Assemblage of cardboard and found objects

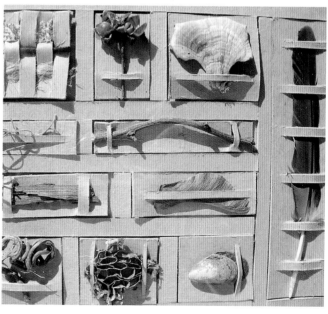

Weaving cardboard and natural materials

The Ochoa Early Childhood Studio

Pauline M. Baker

It was like a
place where only people
who believed in things
could see how
beautiful
things
are.

MARIA HERNANDEZ, fifth grader
posted now on the wall of the
Ochoa Early Childhood Studio,
officially dedicated
on February 17, 2005

The Early Childhood Studio at Ochoa Elementary School is the story of a dream made possible by the energy, hard work, and commitment of many people from many parts of our southern Arizona community, and inspired by the profound and energizing work of the teachers, parents, and children of the municipal schools of Reggio Emilia, Italy.

They have given us a beautiful vision of hope and possibility for young children, which lives in us each day as we collaborate with our children and their families to learn, communicate, and contribute to a democratic way of life.

"It's a Real Rainbow!"

"Es un verdadero arcoiris!" exclaimed Cristian, one of
the children, when he saw the final weaving spread.
The *Color of Our Dreams* weaving reflects all the
colors of the rainbow and offers a vision of what a
small group of people in our southern Arizona early
childhood community wish for the young children
in their lives.

Over many months in 2006, children, parents,
and teachers added lines of colored fiber to create
what has become the first weaving done on the floor
loom in the Peace Garden Early Childhood Studio at
Ochoa Elementary School in Tucson, Arizona.

The Color of Our Dreams weaving speaks with a beauty
that is more than what might be expected of a
collection of fiber and color. It offers a precious and
intimate vision of the hopes and dreams of parents
and teachers for their children, and a glimpse at
the courage and strength of the people who shared
them.

In both the short and long term, we want our child
to grow up with love, health, and well-being.
We want his dreams to guide him.

*A corto y largo plazo queremos para él que crezca con
salud, amor y bienestar son tres cosas importantes para
el desarrollo de cualquier niño. Su suenos queremos
estar con el para guiarlo.*

Small colored cards written in both English and Spanish are attached to this weaving. These cards are inscribed with the hopes and dreams of parents and teachers for the young children in their lives. Cards continue to be added by family members, teachers, and visitors to our school.

We hope that someday this weaving, along with more stories and images telling of the hopes and dreams of families and teachers in Arizona, will be displayed in a traveling exhibit. We dream that this exhibit will command the attention of business leaders and policy makers, and will lead to a greatly improved early learning experience for young children and their families in this state.

A Poem for Literacy

Karen Haigh

Educators in Reggio Emilia consider relationship one of the bases of learning. I find this to be true and powerful in my work, and I want to tell a short story where I see this concept connected with the learning and acquisition of literacy.

In early childhood education, we are lately under pressure to cultivate literacy, seen as essential for the preparation to elementary school. In our program we do not agree with the idea of preparing children for a next step of schooling, but rather we want them to enrich themselves for the present. We find it very important to support their encounter with written language. We are convinced that literacy is of great value seen in terms of communication and expression, not only with the spoken and written language but with many other languages, as the preschools of Reggio showed us.

There are many ways in which children, in their interaction with the environment or preschools, with their peers and the teachers, spontaneously interpret signals and communication that are precursors of literacy.

Teachers, in turn, can construct occasions and experiences that are connected with literacy. In our program, the teachers offer the children illustrated books, and books with words for teachers to read to them.

They create attractive places where children can find all kinds of good paper and a large variety of drawing and painting instruments. They engage children in conversations and transcribe their words, and expect them to draw what they have described or said, extending the scope of oral language into many languages.

"Teacher, I write a poem."

The sky is blue.
The sun is shining like a light.
Candy canes are good and markers are loose,
And diamonds are shiny, just like your ring.

And a teacher is nice just like my teachers.

Angelica, 4½ years old.

Here is the particular story from a preschool classroom:

Angelica, four years old, was intently working with paper and crayons. Her marks seemed very similar to letters; the teacher went closer to the child and asked her what she was doing. The child responded, "Teacher, I write a poem."

Through her relationship with her teacher, Angelica clearly is showing the learning process of developing the ability to make letters. But she also shows that she knows the power of letters to make words to share ideas. She makes connections with the school, the materials, the world outside, and especially with her teacher, all of this portrayed with poetry. Notice how different languages come together: the drawing of flowers, the colors, and the underlined letters in the words of the poem.

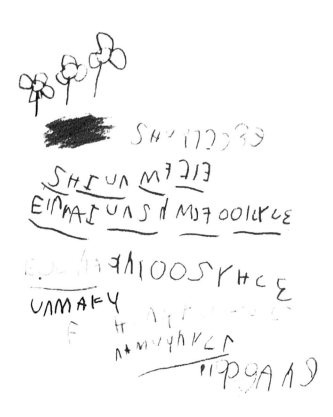

If . . .

Pam Houk

If you help me to
ask my own questions,
try out my ideas,
explore what's around me,
share what I find;

If I have
plenty of time for
my special pace,
a nurturing space,
things to transform;

If you'll be
my patient friend,
trusted guide,
fellow investigator,
partner in learning;

Then I will
explore the world,
discover my voice,
and tell you what I know
in a hundred languages.

One September morning, we sat in a tent in the meadow to observe the insects and animals.

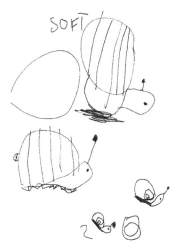

SOFT

Left: Fireflies, birds, butterflies, crickets, bumble-bees, grasshoppers, snails, caterpillars, ants, ladybugs, and worms!

Right: Investigating different sounds by making a sound sculpture.

Designing a play environment for Spikey Bug, a class pet.

The Hundred Languages and Semiotics

Shareen Abramson

According to Loris Malaguzzi, children have a hundred languages for communicating their ideas and cultural understandings. Malaguzzi's philosophy is beautifully distilled in his poem "No way the hundred is there." The poem begins with the affirmation: "The child is made of one hundred/The child has a hundred languages/a hundred hands/a hundred thoughts/hundred ways of thinking/of playing, of speaking."[2] The renowned exhibition, The Hundred Languages of Children, featuring children's work from the schools of Reggio Emilia, Italy, is vivid testimony to the power of children to communicate their thinking, build relationships, and create cultural identity.

The idea of a hundred languages could be a metaphor for children's many capacities for learning, consistent with multiple intelligences theory.[3] However, an alternative explanation of the hundred languages references to an actual theory of language, semiotics, is proposed by the northern Italian linguist Umberto Eco.[4]

Yu, 5.1 years

According to semiotic theory, the sign, a symbol for meaning, is the basis of language and is the constructive element of all communication systems. Any communicative act requires a sign referent (the object, event, or symbol, for example, text) to be represented and a sign interpretant (interpreter) of the meaning given to the sign. In other words, a sign both contains meaning and simultaneously provokes an interpretative response. A sign, for example, a work of art, often has varied meanings resulting from differences in individual perceptions, knowledge, experiences, or context, and this meaning can change over time.

Eco's semiotic theory deals with the linguistic analysis and classification of signs and sign-functions—how signs produce meaning. As a generator of meaning, the sign represents a primary unit of culture, "that system of shared and interconnected meanings that have been organized over time into codes (language, gesture, music, etc.)." Communication is by definition an interactive process that involves interchange with people, the environment, culture, and symbolic systems.[5]

Semiotic theory asserts that there are, literally, many different languages for communication. Providing an all-encompassing theory of language and literacy development, an education in "a hundred languages" has practical applications for developing children's communication abilities. This theory also has special relevance for children whose first language is not English, who benefit educationally and acquire English when afforded broader means for symbolic expression.

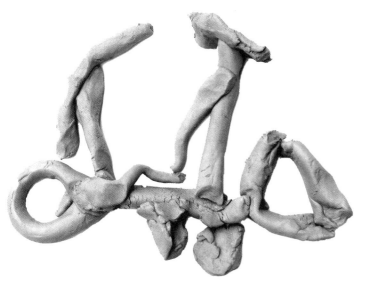

Gabriele, 3.2 years

Mateo, 5 years

Learning these standard systems of communication, including oral and written language, visual and musical codes, and mathematics, leads to communicative literacy, the ability to express ideas symbolically.

Affirming the centrality of language in children's development, as well as its role in learning across the life span, a semiotic interpretation of the hundred languages for achieving communicative literacy offers a new paradigm for reinventing curriculum in today's schools, developing literacy and culture, and strengthening values in an increasingly diverse population here in the United States and in many other countries.

When educational experiences are grounded upon semiotic theory, learners have opportunities to utilize "a hundred languages," a wide repertoire for communicating their ideas. Strategies such as collaborative inquiry, project-based learning, and multimedia documentation provide practical ways to implement semiotic curriculum to develop communicative literacy.[6] Such experiences are highly recommended for English language learners because of their potential to present educationally rich, varied, and challenging content that encourages English language and literacy development, symbolic thinking, social interaction, and cultural awareness. Although still in the process of mastering English, diverse learners are able to see themselves and be seen by their peers and teachers as competent communicators. In recognizing greater possibilities for communicating, students, teachers, and parents build relationships, understand and respect cultural differences, and create shared values. At this time of great public concern over student mastery of language and literacy, communicative literacy developed through a hundred languages is both a means and goal for achieving educational equity and excellence for all.

An Intergenerational Atelier

Lynn Hill

"The atelier was most of all a place for research," [7] Loris Malaguzzi said in an interview with Lella Gandini. The municipally funded preschools and early childhood centers in Reggio Emilia have created an atmosphere that is rich with possibilities for exploration and investigation, integrating emotions, imagination, aesthetics, and cognition into everyday experiences.

These experiences inspired us to transform our own ways of teaching and learning at the Virginia Tech Child Development Laboratory School. The act of looking deeply and seeing things in a new way can be a liberating shift. And opening oneself to the possibility of change can be both challenging and exhilarating.

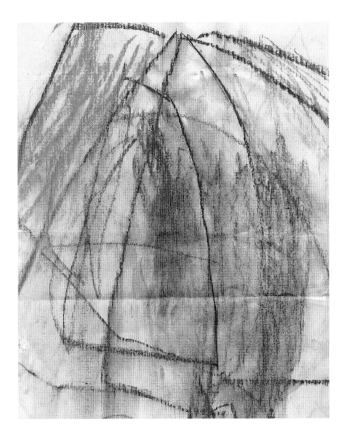

With these reflections in mind, we activated a declaration of intent driven by two research questions:

How might our inspiration and understanding of the Reggio Emilia philosophy be used as a framework to create an intergenerational atelier?

What would be the experience of an older generation interacting with a younger generation through materials in an atelier?

In particular, we imagined the creation of a unique atelier where young children and the older adults, who were spending their days in a connected building, might embark on a journey to construct a very special community.

We challenged one another to be more observant, reflective, and innovative in our research. We acknowledged that our practices before our encounter with Reggio Emilia had been less contemplative and more reactive.

In preparation for this new journey, we carefully reviewed the literature in the area of inter-generational programming and discovered some disappointing findings.

Preschool children were said to have many negative stereotypical attitudes about older people. In addition, most attempts to bring the generations together included the experience of the children performing while the adults quietly observed. How, we asked ourselves, would we find ways to offer more meaningful and respectful ways of being together?

Children and older adults enjoyed an emotional encounter with one another and with the materials in their special atelier.

We recognized that our current intergenerational program reflected many of the research findings, and we were determined to change this. The following year brought a myriad of dilemmas, roadblocks, and questions. But instead of retreating from the challenges, together we found a way to welcome them. The atelier slowly became a source of shared but tentative experiences with materials. Then came some budding friendships between old and young members of the group.

Soon, the children were eagerly awaiting the time of the day when they might visit with the "grandmas and grandpas" (which they were then calling them) in the atelier. In response, the adults began to take on a mentoring role with the children. They delighted in the opportunity to share their wisdom.

After much effort, we were heartened to observe that our reinvented community now offered a strengthened image of both child and adult that led to a more respectful way of honoring its citizens. Strong and affectionate relationships and learning with one another were the result.

A Story of Aesthetics, Relationships, and Care

Before the first fall frost, a flower-salvaging outing was initiated by a former farmer. Children were happy to accept the invitation to harvest the petals from their community garden. The intense color and beauty of the flowers, along with the opportunity to be together, strengthened the relationships between adults and children and increased the possibilities for interaction with natural materials. Later, collaborative drawings and paintings of the flowers enriched the walls of the atelier. And then, a paper-making project extended the life of the blooms.

Time for gentle and sustained exploration of the many materials in the atelier was a gift that we gave ourselves. It was soon evident that the children and the "grandmas and grandpas" were participating as co-researchers in the atelier. Coming together to engage playfully with the materials became a daily experience that was anticipated with pleasure.

Photographs, drawings, short descriptions, and representative materials were gathered and carefully added to a "memory book." The pages of this book were reviewed by the community members on a daily basis. The chance to reminisce in this way served as an important memory-building tool for the older adults and gave a sense of shared history to the group. In addition, the documentation paved the way for new experiences.

The benefits of this special atelier were multiple: the adults displayed a heightened sense of well-being, the children were genuinely comfortable and affectionate with the adults, the positive power of materials was evident, but most of all, we learned that, in the words of Vea Vecchi,

> *"Aesthetics can promote emotions and support empathy with our environment and with one another."* [8]

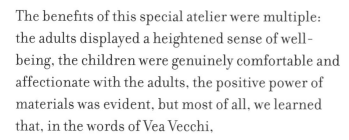

The Dance

Patricia Hunter McGrath

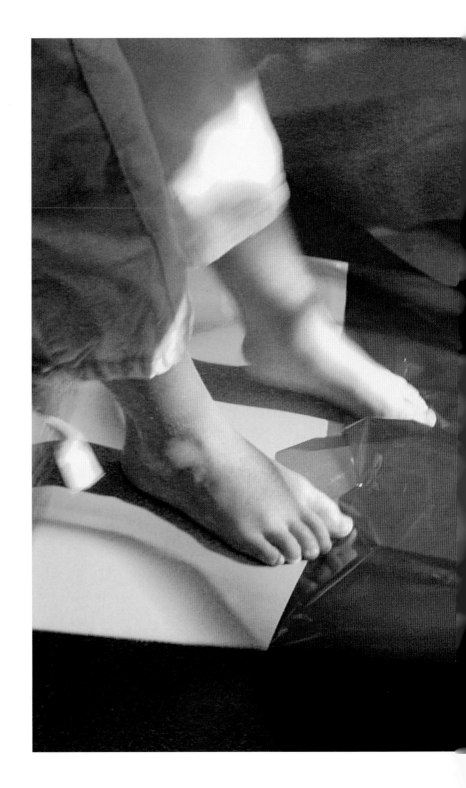

For many years I looked out
   and far away

Seeking but never finding

Somewhere between child and adult

I forgot

I lost

Disconnected

From my heart, imagination,
   and wonder

How could I teach if

I couldn't remember what I had lost

But I couldn't stop searching

I looked out but I couldn't see

What lay at my feet

Waiting for me. . .

Waiting for us. . .

I heard but forgot to listen

Lost

Then one day

A new start

Images of light filled rooms

An abundance of expressive materials

A room full of red poppies

Dancing children

Teachers who listened

A hundred languages to see
   feel and hear

On that day I remembered
    what I had lost

It was there all the time

So I learned to listen

Listen closely

To the children

The children knew

So we started again

They hadn't given up

And the dance began

Children and teacher

Through rooms full of color

Along rivers of clay

Over mountains of paper

To the moon and back

Into the secret worlds of insects,
    flowers, birds and trees

To see the world again in the palm
    of a child's hand

Now I can see

Deep and hidden within me

Wonder

Passion

Joy

Connectedness

All the time it was there

Hidden deep within me . . .

Hidden deep within you . . .

Section Five

The Power of Communication

A meeting at the Model Early Learning Center
on the occasion of the Reggio Emilia Symposium,
organized by Ann Lewin and hosted by The National
Learning Center, in Washington, DC, June 9–12,
1993.

From left: Carolyn Edwards, Lilian Katz, Rebecca
New, Lella Gandini, Baji Rankin, Carlina Rinaldi,
Sergio Spaggiari, Sandra Piccinini, Tiziana
Filippini, Amelia Gambetti, and Loris Malaguzzi

Contributors

CAROLYN POPE EDWARDS writes about the traveling exhibit The Hundred Languages of Children, the impact of the beauty and the content, and the important concepts it teaches us.

PATRICIA WEISSMAN chronicles the start of the periodical, *Innovations in Early Education*, published by Merrill-Palmer in 1992, under the direction of Eli and Rosalyn Saltz.

JUDITH ALLEN KAMINSKY continues to document the history of *Innovations* as a vehicle for communication and exchange among Italian and North American educators. The editors and the board of *Innovations* support the inclusion of writing by those in a variety of Reggio-inspired contexts.

SANDRA MILLER describes the Ohio teachers' exhibit Where Ideas Learn to Fly as a collaborative endeavor that reflects how teachers think and imagine together, and move forward in their practice.

MARGIE COOPER recounts the history of NAREA (North American Reggio Emilia Alliance), an organization made up of educators who invite all of us to engage in advocacy work on behalf of children and childhood.

VICTORIA R. FU's poem reminds us of the multiple possibilities of reinventing the ideas of Reggio Emilia in respectful ways, mindful of context.

SUSAN LYON, starting from the importance of The Hundred Languages of Children exhibit, makes it possible for teachers in a wide local circle in California to exchange ideas and dialogue constructively about issues.

BONNIE NEUGEBAUER, editor of *Exchange Magazine*, discusses the potential within each of us to consider carefully our practice, to change, and to work together thoughtfully.

PAT TARR, also referring to the importance of The Hundred Languages of Children exhibit, uses the metaphor of a web to illustrate the power of interconnectedness and strength one can find in professional community.

LOUISE BOYD CADWELL uses systems theory as a model within the St. Louis-Reggio Collaborative for understanding and developing the ideas of Reggio Emilia.

"Relationship is the primary connecting dimension of our system, however, understood not merely as a warm protecting envelope, but rather as a dynamic conjunction of forces and elements interacting toward a common purpose. The strength of our system lies in the ways we make explicit and then intensify the necessary conditions for relations and interactions. We seek to support those social exchanges that better ensure the flow of expectations, conflicts, cooperations, choices, and the explicit unfolding of problems tied to the cognitive, affective, and expressive realm.

We think of a school for young children as an integral living organism, as a place of shared lives and relationships among many adults and very many children. We think of school as a sort of construction in motion continuously adjusting itself. Certainly we have to adjust the system from time to time while the organism travels on its life course...

It has also always been important to us that our living system of schooling expands toward the world of families, with their right to know and to participate. And then it expands toward the city, with its own life, its own patterns of development, its own institutions, as we asked the city to adopt the children as bearers and beneficiaries of their own specific rights." [1]

LORIS MALAGUZZI

The Inspiration of the Reggio Emilia Exhibit

Carolyn Pope Edwards

The Hundred Languages of Children exhibit tells the story of the educational work in Reggio Emilia. In many ways, it embodies the essence of the philosophy it is describing. For example, it was authored and designed not individually, but through a large ongoing group effort. Loris Malaguzzi always stressed the value of collectivity of time, labor, and ideas. The exhibit demonstrates the quality of results that can come from group work and reciprocity in education.

The exhibit also uses multiplicity, as opposed to simplicity, to make its points. It plunges the visitor into a form of learning that takes place on many levels and through many modalities. Looking at the large, highly detailed panels, densely embedded with words and images, the mind and senses are plunged into a world where impressions pour in on multiple channels, giving the visitor the immediate and tangible experience of learning through "one hundred languages."

Another quality is its circularity. Wandering at will through the exhibit, visitors find themselves on a circular path as they retrace their steps and return repeatedly to favorite panels or themes, each time with deeper understanding. In just this way, education in Reggio Emilia is anything but linear; it is, instead, an open-ended spiral.

The exhibit also shows the value of visibility. The exhibit as a form of communication grew directly out of documentation. Early in their work, Malaguzzi realized that systematically following and sharing the process and results of their work with children would simultaneously serve children, parents, and educators. This bold insight led to the development of documentation as a professional art form in Reggio Emilia. The exhibit makes an integrated statement about the power of documentation.

And finally, the exhibit places a value on incompleteness, or open-endedness. The exhibit never reaches a state where educators say, "Now it is perfect." It continues even to the present day to undergo transformations and emerge in one-after-another versions or editions. In just this way, the educational work in Reggio Emilia never becomes set and routine but instead always undergoes reexamination and experimentation, and resists becoming a model or method.

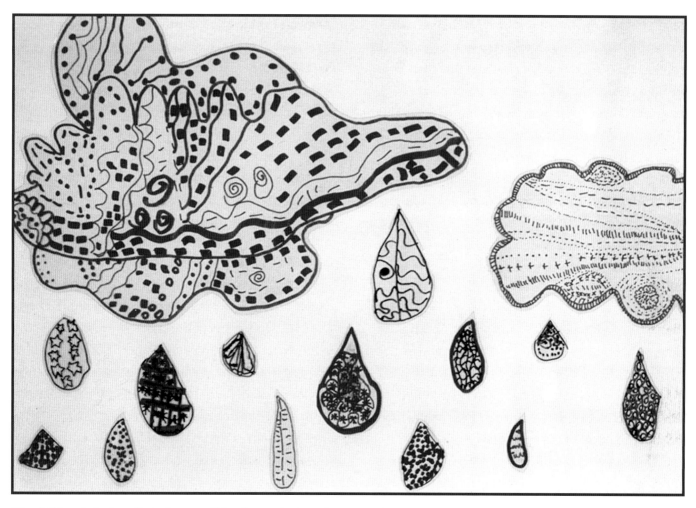

The children's design of raindrops in "The City in the Rain," a project from The Hundred Languages of Children exhibit that first traveled the United States in 1987.

The One Who Became Many

Patricia Weissman with Rosalyn and Eli Saltz

I had the good fortune to be hired at the Merrill-Palmer Institute, a child development research center, at the time that Eli Saltz was director. Although the Saltzes had studied exemplary programs throughout Italy, what they heard about the Reggio schools resonated with them most deeply. They embarked on their own Reggio education—visiting The Hundred Languages of Children exhibit in Boston in 1989, and traveling to Reggio to observe the schools and meet with Reggio educators, including Carlina Rinaldi, pedagogista, and Loris Malaguzzi, founder and philosopher of the Reggio centers.

According to Eli Saltz, "When Loris spoke, it was poetry. When we walked into a Reggio school, it was like walking into a museum. Although the Reggio philosophy emphasizes process over product, the schools were overwhelmingly beautiful." The friendships and discussions that developed in Italy further inspired the Saltzes to devote their professional resources to "transporting" the Reggio approach to the United States. They left Italy with a commitment from Reggio to bring The Hundred Languages exhibit to Detroit in 1991; the exhibit attracted educators from across the country. The Saltzes opened their home to many of the "Reggio pioneers" in the United States, as well as to the Reggio educators Amelia Gambetti, Carlina Rinaldi, and Lella Gandini, to brainstorm ways to disseminate the Reggio approach more widely. It was at the Saltzes' dining room table that the idea of a monthly newsletter was born.

In the fall of 1992, with the generous assistance of our colleagues from Reggio, Reggio liaison Lella Gandini, the advisory committee, and Roz Saltz as associate editor, Merrill-Palmer began publication of *Innovations in Early Education: The International Reggio Exchange*. I served as founding editor. *Innovations* became the bridge between Reggio and educators worldwide. It continues in the capable hands of editor Judith Allen Kaminsky, giving voice to teachers in the United States and Reggio to communicate, collaborate, and learn from each other.

Eli Saltz, Lella Gandini, Rosalyn Saltz, Loris Malaguzzi, and Patricia Weissman, Chicago, May 1993, on the occasion of the award of the Kohl Prize.

In 1993, Loris Malaguzzi made his first trip to the United States to accept the prestigious Kohl International Teaching Award honoring the Reggio Emilia early childhood schools. Loris met with the Saltzes, Lella Gandini, and me to discuss broadening the collaboration between Reggio and North American educators. He expressed his admiration for the beauty and depth of *Innovations* and wished to strengthen the relationship between Reggio and the journal. As he later wrote to Eli, theirs "was a camaraderie going forward."

The many people who generously contributed their ideas, energy, and time to *Innovations* will always be a part of me. By listening to the many perspectives, I have grown both as a teacher and as a person. I came to understand the importance of Carlina's continual entreaty "to listen." Without my exposure to Reggio, I might have gone along my path listening only to my own voice: deciding on my own what would be best for "my kids," working alone in "my" classroom, and viewing those long discussions with colleagues as a waste of my time. Through my many encounters with the Reggio approach and people, I was the one who became many.

Innovations in Early Education:
The International Reggio Exchange
A Symbol of the Value of Collaboration

Judith Allen Kaminsky

The quarterly periodical *Innovations in Early Education: The International Reggio Exchange* has been published by the Merrill-Palmer Institute (MPI), at Wayne State University since 1992. The birth of *Innovations* was inspired by the presence of The Hundred Languages of Children exhibit in Detroit in 1991. At that time, educators from Reggio and the United States participated in a professional development initiative in connection with the exhibit, when the need for a vehicle for dialogue and exchange among Italian and American educators was recognized.

During the next year, Eli Saltz (MPI Director), Rosalyn Saltz (University of Michigan, Dearborn Director of Early Childhood Education), and Patricia Weissman, who would become the editor of *Innovations*, communicated with Loris Malaguzzi and other Reggio educators about the purpose, format, and potential content of the new publication. An editorial board was formed, including the principal American educators in dialogue with the Reggio approach at that time: Carolyn Edwards, George Forman, Lella Gandini, Joanne Hendrick, Lilian Katz, Rebecca New, and Baji Rankin.

Drawings by five-year-old children, La Villetta School, Reggio Emilia.

In the fall of 1992, the first issue of *Innovations* was published. From the beginning, *Innovations* focused on the experiences of Italian and North American educators, who are inspired by the experience and philosophy of the Reggio municipal infant/toddler centers and preschools. In 1994, Amelia Gambetti joined the *Innovations* editorial board and has consistently supported the growth of the relationship between *Innovations* and the Reggio educational community.

In 1997, Lella Gandini became an associate editor, and has been a powerful guiding force in the evolution and integrity of the periodical. The *Innovations* editorial board membership has continued to evolve in order to include the diverse voices of Reggio-inspired educators in North America. In 2000, Paola Riccò joined the editorial board, continuing to work with Amelia Gambetti to facilitate the regular and substantive contributions of Reggio educators to *Innovations*.

Since 1998, each issue of *Innovations* has focused on a particular topic, and has included articles or interviews from the perspective of educators both in Reggio and North America. Due to the strong collaboration of Reggio educators, the interviews and articles represent the experience of many of the pedagogisti, atelieristi, teachers, parents, and community leaders from Reggio. The editors of *Innovations* have also sought to include contributions from a wide array of Reggio-inspired contexts and diverse communities in North America. Because of the consistent quality of the perspectives and experiences shared, *Innovations* has become the resource upon which North American Reggio-inspired educators rely. The editors of *Innovations* are deeply grateful for the ever-evolving collaborative relationship with our Reggio colleagues and look forward to our future work together.

Where Ideas Learn to Fly

Sandra Miller

The title of the Ohio teachers' exhibit, Where Ideas Learn to Fly, is a reference to the identity that is unique to Ohio's history (the Wright brothers and their flying machine) and the intention of a state-wide study group initiative in early childhood education and care.

Giving wings to support children's ideas requires imaginative thinking and intellectual engagement. Providing children with the support, materials, and freedom to be curious, thoughtful, creative, and persistent in their intellectual pursuits comes at the hand of teachers who are given these same considerations. The Ohio teachers' exhibit speaks to the conditions and attitudes needed and desired by children and teachers in realizing their intellectual pursuits, hopes, dreams, and expectations. Giving wings to children's thoughts prepares them to meet the future with the confidence in their efficacy as learners and producers of knowledge.

Our inspiration for learning how to support children's theories and ideas taking flight comes from studying the theory and understanding the values of the work of the educators of Reggio Emilia. In our visits to the schools of Reggio Emilia, we saw firsthand the reality and results of these values.

On one such trip we captured the words of Ohio teachers who were inspired by walking through the schools, examining the environment, and reading the documentation:

creative

democratic

emotional

flexible

forgiving

honest

intellectual

intentional

reciprocal

reflective

respectful

supportive

transparent

Teachers participating in the Ohio study group desire to create an atmosphere where ideas, hopes, and aspirations become a reality for all of our children, regardless of setting, and as we work together, to demonstrate these values in action with our children and with each other.

Where Ideas Learn to Fly

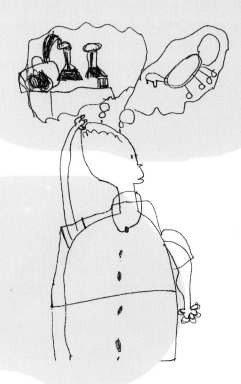

"The brain holds the air so you can talk like when it's cold outside and the air comes to your mouth. Ideas come from your brain. Your brain helps you change your ideas."

- Jermaine, age 5

Sponsored by the Ohio Department of Education, Office of Early Learning and School Readiness, with support from the Martha Holden Jennings Foundation.

Not Just a Place but an Idea

Margie Cooper

The city of Reggio Emilia is not only a place of its own citizens, but a hometown for all whose passion is the welfare of young children. And the city is not just a place, but an idea—an idea that gives birth to new ideas.

NAREA (North American Reggio Emilia Alliance) is but one of these offspring ideas, conceived in the exchange of thought among many. We are permanently grateful to those whose work in the defense and promotion of children's rights built the foundation of this idea now known as NAREA. We remember with gratitude Loris Malaguzzi, who in a 1993 letter to Lilian Katz, translated by Lella Gandini, wrote:

With regard to the United States, what we look forward to (and I know it is not easy) is friendship, accompanied by an organized form of solidarity, with plans of action more coordinated and efficient...We know that there are several interested friends and institutions, and it would be good to have a project that connects together autonomous institutions and people,

all in the United States, through a diversified program of initiatives having in common a thread of friendship toward Reggio. It would be important not to exclude anyone, and everyone should participate.

For more than a decade before NAREA was formed in North America, there were contributions of time and effort by numerous U.S. educators to create the project that Malaguzzi described. Canada and Mexico, too, have a rich collection of historical efforts that have given rise to current levels of interest in this work of our time.

Today, NAREA is an organization of activist advocates who "envision a world where all children are honored and respected for their potential, capabilities, and humanity," an organization that seeks to make childhood an exceptional experience for all.

gio Emilia Alliance

Images of Multiplicity

Victoria R. Fu

We are Travelers, explorers
in search of what could be.[2]
From the Appalachians to the Adirondacks,
Allegheny Plateau, Smokey Mountains,
Great Plains, Great Lakes . . .
From the land of Lonesome Pines, dogwood,
sugar maple, paper birch, tulip poplar . . .
Images of Multiplicity.

Crossing the ocean,
over the mountains to Reggio Emilia:
A seed was planted in the Travelers' minds.
Provoking us to take another look at
the aesthetics of teaching and learning,
in our search of what could be.

"You have to make it your own"
Echoed in our minds.
Challenging and inviting
us to reinvent, reconstruct—recast.
Make relevant what could be in
our Land of Multiplicity.
A landscape traversed by people
of many colors and voices in
a Hundred Languages and many, many more...
Ever changing, ever provoking,
Searching for ways to
teach and learn in our own ways.

The Travelers discovered the essence of
self-reflection in one's situated life,
to be open to the plurality of other lives,
to change, transform, and recast.

Recasting learnings from Reggio Emilia
takes root in this Land of Multiplicity.
Social and political changes open doors
to a world of imagination and possibilities.
Recasting anew,
seeing through different eyes,
creating thousands of images of reality—
Images of multiplicity.

Lonesome Pines, dogwood,
    sugar maple, paper birch, tulip poplar…
Spirally through the seasons,
the Travelers are revitalized with
new questions to provoke,
new answers to discover.
What could be in our Land of
Multiplicity and possibilities.

The Innovative Teacher Project
The Power of Exchange and Dialogue

Susan Lyon

In California, The Hundred Languages of Children exhibit from Reggio Emilia, Italy, has been the catalyst for dialogue and exchange between educators, creating a project that evolved into a network of schools. It inspired educators and parents to become more attentive, to do more, to be more with children, to be more with one another. The exhibit became a catalyst for new discussions, affirming awareness and joy in children's potential and the potential of schools to develop deeper learning and relationship.

The exhibit is a reflection of the schools of Reggio Emilia, and a reflection of how theory and practice are bridged in those schools with joy, care, and education. Images, narratives, sculptures in wire and clay, drawings, paintings, collages, children's conversations, and teachers' interpretations all work together in the exhibit toward helping us to pay close attention to the power of exchange and dialogue.

The exhibit marked the beginning of my journey. I found a strong encouragement and an extra-ordinary perspective for looking at my work through different lenses. I am fortunate to have had an opportunity to share the exhibit with so many people from all over the world.

The exhibit was the inspiration for The Innovative Teacher Project, a nonprofit organization that initiates and supports roundtables among schools and ongoing professional development, inspired by the Reggio approach to early childhood education. Since 1994, many schools, teachers, educators, administrators, professors, parents, and children have contributed and participated in The Innovative Teacher Project. This network of educators and schools is a source of encouragement and hope for the future for children and families.

I am deeply aware and appreciative of all the wonderful colleagues and friends from Reggio Emilia and around the world who have come to work with us these past years.

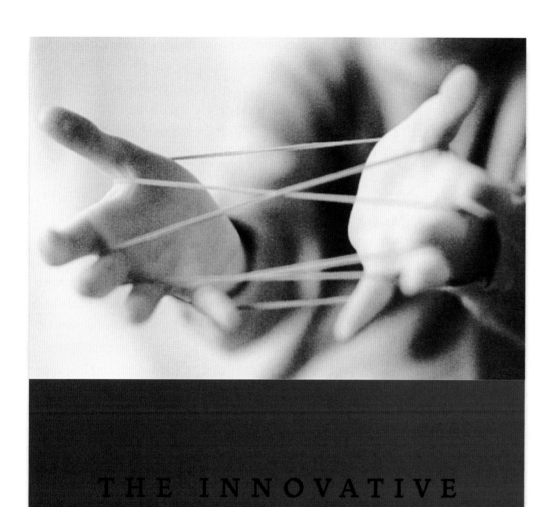

THE INNOVATIVE

TEACHER

PROJECT

Unpacking My Questions and Images
Personal Reflections on Reggio Emilia

Bonnie Neugebauer

When I visited the schools for young children in Reggio Emilia, Italy, I expected to learn about an exemplary educational system, but I began to glimpse a different way of living.

I had carefully secured the doorstop in my mind, a secure (or so I thought) place from which to hold on to my reservations. I did not want to be blown out of my comfort zone. But as conversations and days passed, the flood of impressions and ideas not only moved the doorstop—they tore the door from its hinges.

Reggio Emilia is a place where children come first. They don't come first after budget constraints or staffing issues or anything else. They simply, and significantly, come first. Everything centers around them and evolves through them. They are the focus of all that happens. You not only see and hear this message as you enter the schools, you feel it, even taste it. This is their place, a place that bears the stamp of their individual personalities, their learning experiences, and their own particular community at work. The presence and work of children permeates the space.

Teachers appear to be on the alert for creating moments and occasions that will surprise or delight the children. There is a sense of excitement. This is a place where surprises can happen and an unplanned, unbidden event can change the course of the day.

It would be difficult, perhaps impossible, for us to try to replicate the Reggio schools in the United States. But it would be foolish to miss or reject the opportunity to learn from them. Whether we intensely study what they have done, or whether we visit Italy briefly or attend their seminars here, or whether we read about what they are doing, each of these experiences is an opportunity to change, to look at what we are doing, and to work and live more thoughtfully.

Teachers and toddlers observing together.

The Hundred Languages of Children Exhibit in Calgary

Pat Tarr

1994–1997

A pebble drops

An idea

Ripples out

Capturing imagination

Creating community

1997–2005

Ariadne's thread connects us,[3]

Binds us

A spider's web of relationships

Striving, struggling,

Nurturing community

2006

Indra's net spread against the sky

Each jeweled juncture

Reflecting and refracting journeys

Macrocosms, microcosms interconnected

Strengthening community

The key messages in text and image in The Hundred Languages of Children exhibit tells of the potential of relationships and the power of community to create possibilities.

Hosting the exhibit twice in Calgary has strengthened our relationships and our community of Reggio-inspired educators in ways that we are just beginning to understand as we near the end of the exhibit's residency.

A pebble drops

Twelve years ago, when a group of people met with the goal of bringing the exhibit to Calgary in 1997, few others in the area had heard of Reggio Emilia. "Reggio who?" was a typical question. The presence of the exhibit for two months in the fall of 1997 created the beginning of the local Reggio-inspired community. Two conferences created ripples that began to move beyond our regional borders as we entered into dialogues with Reggio-inspired educators from across North America.

The spider's web

Now the group becomes larger and we begin to weave a spider's web, supporting each other in our quest to construct our understanding of "the image of the child," of ourselves as educators, of parents, and of our teaching environments. Developing understanding of materials as a language plays a predominant part of this journey. The web connects outside of the area as more people travel to other places, including Reggio Emilia, to deepen their understanding.

Indra's Net

The experience of hosting the exhibit in 2006 has been very different from 1997, when two museums and their staffs dealt with many of the exhibition details, including installation. We have now become intimately acquainted with the exhibit through involvement with each aspect of installing, deinstalling, and reinstalling the exhibit, and planning and hosting related professional development activities. Relationships have become broadened and have become more interwoven. Our involvement has increased and strengthened our own community, uncovered and developed new leaders, shown us our ability to realize dreams, and unveiled new possibilities. We feel more deeply connected to others on a similar journey. Each encounter has contributed to who we are becoming. Our experience has become one of the myriad experiences reflected in the surfaces of Indra's net,* in which each is part of and reflects the whole. For this opportunity we are deeply grateful.

*Indra's net—also called Indra's jewels or Indra's pearls—
is a Buddhist metaphor for the interconnectedness all things.

A Hundred Languages, a Hundred Connections—and More

Angela Ferrario

My first encounter with Reggio Emilia was in 1989. I responded to a request in the Boston Association for the Education of Young Children newsletter from a local early childhood educator, Baji Rankin, asking for volunteers interested in bringing The Hundred Languages of Children exhibit to Boston. The majority who formed the exhibit host group in Boston became part of the first delegation to Reggio Emilia that I helped organize in 1990. There were twenty-three participants. Seventeen years later, following the creation of Reggio Children in 1994 and the recently established Loris Malaguzzi International Center, I am grateful to remain in the role of U.S. Liaison for Study Groups to Reggio Emilia.

Jan Millikan, a professor at University of Melbourne, also registered for the 1990 delegation when she heard about it by chance. Soon after, as interest in the Reggio philosophy was growing in Australia, Jan became the Reggio Emilia reference point for Australia. Several years later, in July 2006, I sat with Jan and others representing countries around the world as we came together with Reggio educators at the Loris Malaguzzi International Center to launch the International Reggio Children

Network. It was the dream of Loris to have such a network that would support the work of teachers and children in many countries as a collaborative effort and to see that borders could be crossed through the sharing of deep convictions about the potentials of all children.

My role has grown and changed as delegations of twenty-five became study tours of one hundred and study tours grew into international study groups of four hundred. There are now regional and multistate study groups to Reggio Emilia for educators who have been working together and have been in dialogue with the Reggio experience for a long period of time. When Baji moved from Boston to New Mexico, she forged new collegial relationships and collaborations with other Reggio-inspired educators, who are now part of a multistate study group.

Over the years, my life has been influenced by the Reggio philosophy. In my work particularly, the value of relationships and working together in a collegial manner has held major significance. The value of organization is another fundamental aspect of the work in Reggio that has become relevant to my role as liaison. Seeing organization as a value is integral to successful study group experiences.

The Boston Group at Anna Frank School, June 1990.

International Study Tour Group, May/June 2005.

A group of colleagues and I, involved in Reggio-inspired work throughout the United States, Canada, and Mexico, founded NAREA (North American Reggio Emilia Alliance) in 2002. The initiatives of NAREA are now multifaceted and are always rooted in our first connections with Reggio. In fact, for example, Alba DiBello, a 1990 delegation participant, is now one of sixty-four NAREA membership coordinators.

Because of my collegial relationships with Barbara Acton, Executive Director of Childhood League Center in Ohio, and Sharon Palsha, Professor at University of North Carolina (early delegation participants), I was able to call upon them to be speakers at the 2007 NAREA Summer Conference. Without ever having met each other, both willingly agreed to be co-presenters on a panel entitled "Evolutions in the Inclusion of Children with Special Rights." Barbara and Sharon were introduced via conference call, and as they developed their presentation in collaboration they also developed a strong collegial relationship driven by the common bond of the Reggio inspiration.

As I consider these few examples, I realize how they symbolize the hundreds of connections, relationships, and collaborative projects that have stemmed from groups formed around a common interest in the Reggio philosophy—especially from those initial encounters made among participants during delegations/study groups to Reggio Emilia, the city that opened its schools to offer us new learning experiences.

Systems Thinking   A Worldview

Louise Boyd Cadwell

In *Schools that Learn*, Peter Senge discusses the "systems revolution," which asserts that "the fundamental nature of reality is relationships not things." Senge predicts that the "systems revolution" will eventually work its way into our worldview, replacing Newtonian, mechanistic thinking and industrial-age schools where knowledge and skills are often taught in fragmented ways outside of a meaningful context.[4] Loris Malaguzzi was drawn to the ideas of early systems-thinkers Gregory Bateson, Humberto Maturana, and Francesco Varela. Systems thinking takes its place among the ideas that Malaguzzi courageously translated across disciplines into a living pedagogy that has been in evolution ever since.

The worldview that frames much of our work in the schools of the St. Louis-Reggio Collaborative is not fragmented into pieces and parts. Rather, it is steeped in context and meaning making; it is whole, dynamic, and relational. If we are able to clearly articulate our values, our worldview, and our beliefs about the essential place of "making meaning" in our lives, and then demonstrate how this unfolds in the stories of children's and teachers' experiences, we will not only reach the parents of the children whom we teach, we will also begin to stand for and speak from, as author Fritjof Capra, says, "a new vision of reality that is ecological."[5] I am quite sure this is what the Italians mean when they say that in acting out our lives as teachers in this way, we are taking a political stance; we are standing for a way of being that is outside the norm and that is ultimately crucial to the future of the planet.

Together, all of us have entered a new millennium, one which holds promise and one in which we face enormous global challenges. I carry with me a deep and profound hope that the wisdom of this small, vibrant city in the north of Italy will continue to have a huge effect on our thinking and our practice in education. I pray that it may also continue to inspire us to understand ourselves as a piece of a universe in which all parts are connected and linked to the past and to the future.

June 6 '92. 6 AM.

This morning our piazza is cool. a darkening range of gray clouds to the south west. a breeze. after yesterday's strong wind. I hear the strong flapping of the pigeons as they take off. flap flap flap flap. I hear a shutter open. stretching and clanking. probably its Teresa. The constant mantra of the morning doves- coo coo coo , coo coo coo. The rumble of the train pulling out or passing by Reggio. and the higher guttural calling of the pigeon? Then the high screech of the swallows. and swifts who fly and swoop high above. Sailing on the air currents? a sparrow + merlo streak by on the way to the nearest park sycamore.

The tomato soup building was brilliantly lit this morning with the rising sun before it ducked behind these banks of clouds. They gray side of another lit (with the)+ shadowed with shape of the building in front of it. . . . The first bus rumbles / thunders by. a high train whistle. wee . . . . toot toot. . and then the train sound . I think of getting on that train. headed for France. we'll be excited to see Ashley I know.

I see these swallows for miles - They are everywhere . a few people have walked slowly across the piazza. The forno is open. this piazza is so familiar. tiled patches of rooves. fitting together like puzzle pieces. two towers of San Francesco. Mrs. Paches. Geraniums. the arbori (?) the tall trees of the gardens. The imposing tomato red facade of our companion apartment building. windows like so many eyes. shutters like eyelids. . . . . small patch of blue. over the tower .

History and Civic Awareness: Building Environments and Communities

Seminar in Reggio Emilia, June 1994

Although Loris Malaguzzi died in February 1994, the international seminar that he had envisioned went ahead as planned in June 1994 because of the determination of Carlina Rinaldi and colleagues as a tribute to the continuing vitality of what he had accomplished.

Contributors

Jeanne Goldhaber revisits the development of the interest in Reggio Emilia that has transformed the work with students, teachers, and children at the University of Vermont Children's Center, and the connections often forgotten with the philosophy of John Dewey.

Mary Mumbrue also speaks about the importance of becoming aware of the history of one's particular context, as she recounts the history of her own school founded by Carleton Washburne of the Progressive Education Movement.

Susan Etheredge and Martha Lees write about the process of constructing a new early childhood school building at Smith College, highlighting the intentionality of the design decisions as inspired by Reggio principles and practices. They begin as our colleagues in Reggio do, by reconsidering the history of their place and space.

Andrew Stremmel, Kay Cutler, and Laura Gloege narrate the story of a collaborative endeavor to design a playground that chronicles how collaborative, active inquiry and investigation have transformed their school into a vital community for all.

Mary Hartzell and Joanne Mandakas tell us a story about preschool children becoming members of the community as they explore and investigate the Third Street Promenade, a popular walk-street in their city of Santa Monica, California.

Lynne Brill and Kim Lee Ripley speak about the inspiration they have received from Reggio to consider carefully how young children construct identity and culture. They describe how the outdoor environment of their school engages children in developing a sense of self and a sense of place.

J. Ronald Lally, after a trip to Reggio Emilia, and with the teachers who are studying with him, discovers how infants and toddlers are seen as part of the community in that city. Two of the teachers experiment in their local context, based on what they have learned from Reggio.

Dianna Smith looks at the hidden abilities of toddlers and, with the student teachers, follows the toddlers, observing closely their way of making choices and becoming a group.

Ellen Hall lists the rights of children as articulated by them through the declaration of the Boulder Journey School, helping children to see themselves as citizens.

John Nimmo writes about conflicts among children, which are not always negative but a necessary experience and source of growth.

David Fernie reflects on the power of professional community to support us as we seek to understand better contemporary challenge and change.

John Dewey, who has been a source of inspiration for progressive education in both Italy and the United States, believed that over time, people engaged in repeated and varied experiences to learn more about each other, build common interests, and commit energy based on awareness of a shared future. Community stretches beyond a static life in the present to include a complex interaction of memories of the past, events in the present, and hopes for the future…The image of the child in Reggio Emilia is one that places the child within the context of history—both personal, lived history and the heritage of one's culture and society. Loris Malaguzzi made this point eloquently on one of his visits to the United States:

"We have to think in the plural—the children, the people. Each of us contains many people. I contain many people, you contain many people. Children are like a big bowl of soup—they contain lots of pieces of history and are a continuous reconstruction of that history."

Educators in Reggio Emilia talk frequently about the importance of "continuity" in children's lives and use many practices to support that notion…Documentation provides a concrete memory of adults' and children's lives together…and rituals and celebrations are used to mark the passage of time in a way accessible to children.[1]

JOHN NIMMO

To Italy and Back A Teacher Education Program's Journey

Jeanne Goldhaber

I wonder what the past fifteen years would have been like if in 1991 several of us had not joined a delegation of thirty-five early childhood educators to observe and learn about the infant/toddler programs and preschools of Reggio Emilia. An interesting question, given the sometimes subtle, sometimes overarching ramifications that single decision has had on our early childhood teacher education program and lab school at the University of Vermont. While we, like most visitors to Reggio Emilia after their first visit, were driven to make immediate changes to our environment, we soon decided to focus our attention on documentation. We thought that documentation would support us in our efforts to prepare our students to be better observers and that it would contribute to our students' ability to plan curriculum based on observation. In retrospect, I am amused and not a little embarrassed by the naïveté of this decision. However, I fear that had we understood the extent to which our study of documentation was going to influence our identity and belief system as a teacher education program and lab school, we never would have dared to begin!

But begin we did, bolstered by a shared constructivist perspective and, as importantly, good friendships. We brought our thinking into our undergraduate courses and practica, and both our growing understanding and misunderstanding of documentation were mirrored in our students' work. Our thinking about documentation evolved slowly, moving from a static and concrete conceptualization to a more active and abstract one, until we came to see ourselves and our students as not only educators but as teacher-researchers as well. Indeed, this decade-long study of documentation has led to a fundamental shift in our thinking about children and pedagogy, and ultimately to a belief that these two concepts are, in fact, inextricable.

Perhaps an example would be helpful. With our transformation from a morning preschool to a full-day, year-round school for children from six weeks to five years old in 1990, we are a relatively young program. When planning the spaces for the different groups of children, we were concerned about having infants in a building that not only contains our center, but also the hustle and bustle of student residential suites, classrooms, and offices. Upon reflection, I see these concerns as reflecting our then culturally embedded and as yet unexamined view of very young children as fragile and in need of protection from what we then saw as a potentially overstimulating, overwhelming outside world.

Indeed, had we not decided to apply our evolving understanding of documentation as a cycle of inquiry to investigate the nature of the infants' relationships with the preschoolers, I suspect that we would have continued to communicate to our undergraduates the necessity of "keeping the babies safe" by our initial practice of limiting their experiences to the materials and relationships of their small and self-contained classroom

environment. Instead, as we documented the developing relationships between the infants and preschoolers, we observed again and again evidence of their intense interest in the world outside their classroom's door—and the world's reciprocal interest in them.

That small step—or rather those many small steps—that carried our babies outside their classroom propelled us to more observation and yet another level of reflection about our children in their community. Our students and their mentor teachers shared their documentation of the preschoolers' efforts to welcome the new babies to the center by making mobiles for the infant room. We took note of the economic acumen, entrepreneurial spirit, and sheer force of will of the children, the preschool "leaders," as they spent the summer on our downtown pedestrian mall selling their handmade paper to buy a tire swing for the incoming preschool class. Is it possible that had we not allowed our eyes to "jump over the wall" to consider the possibility that children are both able and eager to contribute to the well-being of their community, our undergraduate students—tomorrow's teachers—might never have had the opportunity to learn of children's potential engagement as citizens and ambassadors of democracy?

Today, our undergraduates routinely accompany the babies as they make their daily visits to other classrooms. They observe and document the children's encounters with the minstrels and street merchants, teenagers and elders, tourists, pigeons, and puppies that populate our city during our much anticipated summer months. They expect the toddlers and preschoolers to respond enthusiastically to an invitation to help care for the turtles in our lakefront science museum and beautify it with plantings and flowers. And, indeed, they do.

It is clear to me that our program's study of documentation has shaped our teacher education program and lab school in fundamental and profound ways. We see ourselves as generating knowledge, knowledge that informs our thinking about children, learning, and pedagogy, and their collective and active role in the creation and nurturing of community. We try to offer our students the perspective of teacher research and the tools of documentation with which to challenge the unconscious and yet powerful lens that we develop by virtue of our personal, cultural, and sociopolitical contexts.

It is perhaps ironic that we had to cross the Atlantic to rediscover Dewey, a native of Vermont, who argues that good schooling is fundamental to the creation and nurturance of a democracy. Would we have arrived at this point in our thinking about the rights and responsibilities of citizenship as not only a birthright but also as beginning at birth without the tools of documentation? Would we have arrived at a belief in our own and our students' potential as researchers and meaning makers without profiting from the insights and knowledge that the process of inquiry promotes? Perhaps we needed to embark on our own journey—a journey that brought us to Italy and back—to recognize our own cultural bias and genius, to question our values and reclaim our educational legacy, to celebrate our mistakes, and hope for more. Indeed, as teacher educators, we hope that each of our students will enter the profession with the curiosity of a researcher, eager to learn what the children have to teach them about the world, and the role and responsibility we all have in its creation.

Crow Island School History and Continuity

Mary Mumbrue

I picked up a copy of *Young Children* in September 1990 only because of the title on the cover, "Excellent Early Education: A City in Italy Has It," written by Rebecca New. Until that time, I had only a cursory interest in early childhood education, as I am a middle grades elementary school teacher. My reason for even reading the article by Rebecca New in *Young Children* was that Reggio Emilia was the area where my grandfather was born and an area where our family still resides.

This serendipitous selection began my transformation as a teacher and introduced me to philosophical ideas and environmental design that I had not considered before.

I became intrigued with the Reggio Emilia early childhood philosophy because it seemed like a natural extension of the philosophy already in place in Winnetka. The Winnetka, Illinois, public school system has embraced the Progressive Education philosophy since the early days of its founding by Carleton Washburne. The type of educational experiences that Dewey was looking to establish in schools has long been a part of my District #36. So, soon after reading the article in *Young Children* and in my role as Director of the Winnetka Teachers' Institute, I contacted Rebecca New, Lella Gandini, George Forman, and Carolyn Pope Edwards, who agreed to present at an Institute Day in Winnetka about the Reggio Emilia schools.

Inside the classroom

In 1992, I had the fortune to see firsthand the schools of Reggio as one of only sixteen participants in an early delegation. Then, the next year on a return trip to Reggio, I had the opportunity to observe Eva Tarini, a first grade teacher at Crow Island School in Winnetka, while she was an intern in the Reggio Emilia preschools. At the time of this second visit, Loris Malaguzzi generously invited me to walk around by myself in the various centers to observe as well as sit in on the staff meetings. That gave me the unusual opportunity to see the benefits of many of the practices in Reggio Emilia and to observe a most effective documentation process that became for me a living daily project.

First grade children check messages in the mailboxes

Since that Institute Day in 1991, the Winnetka public schools have hosted other Reggio educators, such as Amelia Gambetti and Carlina Rinaldi. The most extraordinary visit for us was the one when Loris Malaguzzi spent time with us in District #36 when he was in Chicago to accept an international award from the Kohl Foundation.

My perception, over the years, has been that while we, as elementary school teachers, learned to develop pedagogical documentation and captured the story of the children's experience and understandings, we pursued our own learning through reflection and research. The philosophy of Reggio Emilia has sustained our collective curiosity, imagination, collaboration, and resourcefulness as educators.

Crow Island School

Space as Connection and Transformation

Susan Etheredge and Martha Lees

"It is our vision that each child who comes through our door joins a community of children, families, and teachers engaged in the joy, work, and wonder of childhood."

Vision Statement,
Center for Early Childhood Education,
Smith College

The Smith College Center for Early Childhood Education is located on the Fort Hill campus of Smith College in Northampton, Massachusetts. The program offers full- and part-time early education and care for children, infancy through preschool, and is open to all children in the surrounding communities. The center is commonly referred to as "Fort Hill." Fort Hill refers to the land that English settlers offered as shelter to the local Nonotuck Indians upon attack by Mohawk Iroquois Indians from the west in 1664, a decade after Northampton was founded.

The Fort Hill early childhood program was established in 1926 by the president of Smith College to provide educational opportunities for Smith College graduate students.

The program was housed in an elegant mansion that was built in 1838 by Samuel Whitmarsh, who introduced silk manufacturing to Northampton. The property was surrounded with gardens, shrubbery, trees, walks, and a greenhouse, and was one of the most beautiful places in the Connecticut River Valley. It was featured in mid-nineteenth-century tourist guides as the perfect place for a carriage ride. The Whitmarsh property was then bought by Catherine and Edward Lyman in 1866 to use as a summer home. The estate remained in the Lyman family until 1946, when Smith College purchased the property.

Throughout the twentieth century, the early childhood program continued to grow and provide a laboratory for the departments of education and psychology, offering opportunities for Smith College students and faculty to conduct research and educate student teachers. As the childcare needs of Smith employees increased, the program expanded to offer full-day, full-year programs and care for infants and toddlers, as well as preschoolers. By 2004, there were seven early childhood classrooms housed in the Lyman home and in three apartments, which were part of an apartment complex (circa 1960) on the property. These apartments, located across the field, provided rental housing to members of the college community.

The distance between the main building and the apartments, as well as the layout of the classrooms, created both a physical and psychological separation. The Lyman home also presented a number of additional challenges, including issues with lead paint and aging mechanical systems. After an extensive review of the program and the property, the college decided to build a new early childhood center and a building committee was formed. The committee determined that a major goal for the new center was to build a space that would house all the classrooms and would support cohesion and invite collaboration.

After reviewing several sites, the committee began planning for a new building in the field between the mansion and the apartments.

Fort Hill, housed in the historic Lyman estate until 2005

In designing the new building, we turned to Reggio Emilia for inspiration. For many years, Fort Hill teachers had been studying the ideas of Reggio Emilia through their relationship with Lella Gandini, U.S. Liaison for the Dissemination of the Reggio Emilia Approach, a Smith alumna and resident of Northampton. The following design principles, developed by architects and teachers in Reggio Emilia, guided the intentionality of our design choices for the new school environment, pictured here.[2]

Overall softness: to create an amiable place, livable and serene.

A relational space: to invite connection, communication, and collaboration between and among children and adults.

Children exploring the Smith College Botanic Garden

Continuity with surroundings, environments, and social connections: to cultivate enriching relationships with the neighborhood, college, and the community.

Flexibility and adaptation: to have a space for learning that can be easily modified to respond to children's initiations and needs.

The Common is a place for exploring, moving, gathering, and collaborating. It was inspired by the piazza in Reggio Emilia and translated to reflect our own cultural context and the town common, a traditional feature of New England towns.

Community and participation: to construct a space that supports dialogue, reciprocity, and exchange among children, teachers, and parents.

The Smith College Center for Early Childhood Education at Fort Hill, present day.

The documentation "Exploring Light, Color, and Shadow" reflects the remaining four principles that guided our design choices and continue to guide our daily practice to this day.

Multiple sensorial experiences: to invite children to discover reality through sensorial explorations, and construct their knowledge and memory through them.

The school as a laboratory: to create learning spaces (with a variety of materials and tools) that inspire and invite children to engage in active and dynamic investigations.

Narration: to communicate, through multiple ways, children's learning, to make visible what children understand and how they make meaning.

Rich normality: to achieve in the space a sense of well-being, generated by harmony, equilibrium, and positive interactions of different elements— an intense richness as a normal shared expectation, rather than an exceptional occurrence. As Carlina Rinaldi writes, such a space "creates an environment that is pleasant to be in, that can be explored and experienced with all the senses, and inspires further advancements in learning: an environment that is empathetic, that grasps the meaning of, but also gives meaning to, the life of the people who inhabit it."[3]

We find that while the new school building may hold less grandeur than the original Lyman mansion, the sense of community we have achieved in the new space holds its own grandeur.

The East Room: Exploring Light, Color, and Shadow

A documentation created by Kelly Blondin, teacher of toddlers

The East Room children continue to be captivated by shadow-making and projected color, and their interest has only been deepened by the inclusion of the overhead projector and shadow screen into our room.

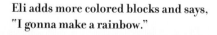

They search the room and choose objects to try out on the projector—looking at them first on the projector's surface and then turning to see the images on the screen. Michael moves the transparent colored blocks, then chooses foam letters from a puzzle. He points to the letter B and says, "B!" He then turns to look at the B on the screen and shouts, "Hey, it's a big B. A shadow B!"

Eli adds more colored blocks and says, "I gonna make a rainbow."

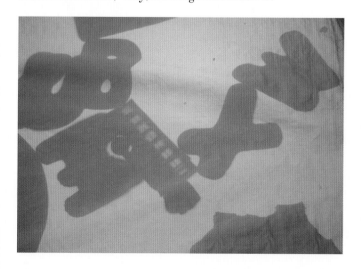

Designing a Playground A Collaborative Investigation

Andrew Stremmel, Kay Cutler, and Laura Gloege

At South Dakota State University, the early childhood education faculty is committed to studying and recasting the Reggio Emilia approach. Since 2001, we have embarked on a journey of relationship building, reflection, and self-understanding that has included the infusion of Reggio-inspired, inquiry-based learning into children's experiences and the early childhood teacher education program. As we have learned from the educators of Reggio Emilia, we cannot educate children and educate ourselves in isolation, only in a community of people who value exchange and dialogue and, therein, find the origins of curiosity and the desire to learn. Education takes place through relationships, which often do not leave traces of what is essential, so we must make these visible.

Documentation brings to life what usually escapes our eyes and helps teachers discover what is involved in children's learning processes.

Most recently our efforts have focused on renovating and expanding our laboratory preschool and kindergarten. The Fishback Center for Early Childhood Education was completed in fall 2006, and the redesigning of the existing playground will fully complete this state-of-the-art center.

We describe briefly with images our strategy for how we came to think and talk about the design of an "environments playground." This project created an ongoing dialogue among children and the university students from early childhood education and landscape design, as well as among teachers, parents, faculty, and staff. The children's ideas were clearly included to give them a sense of ownership in the process. We invited them to cooperate with the student teachers who asked the children, "If you could choose anything you wanted, what would you put on in the playground?"

Here are some of the children's suggestions:

> *more slides*
>
> *monkey bars*
>
> *swings with stuff to swing on*
>
> *paths to drive cars and sleds on, and train tracks*
>
> *There should be lights so they can go out and play at night.*

The investigation by the young children with their teachers was launched.

As the children engaged in drawing and exchanging ideas, the landscape and design students engaged in a parallel exchange across campus. They also began their investigation by listening carefully as they interviewed the children and parents, examining their ideas, learning about the center's philosophy, and talking with the teachers.

The students began to design an outdoor learning space that incorporated our context's identity, provided open-ended learning spaces, created natural spaces for varying groups of children, and included many of the thoughts and ideas of children and parents.

Each day the children and teachers determined together who would work on which aspect of the investigation. The children jointly transformed their ideas into three-dimensional constructions. When the teachers revisited the documentation, they noticed that the children drew upon each other's strengths, even walking around and giving advice to others.

When working on a blueprint of their playground space, a small group of children negotiated the placement of pieces. A teacher asked, "How do we decide where the pond goes?" There were many different opinions: "Have three ponds." "So I can fish and the pond can be in the middle because it is perfect." "If it is in the middle it will all sink." (He wanted the pond by the swing and monkey bars.)

Some children showed concern about children of different ages playing around the pond and its location. If the pond was near any of the equipment or the hill, the toddlers might fall in, some thought. Others suggested that the toddlers must wear lifejackets.

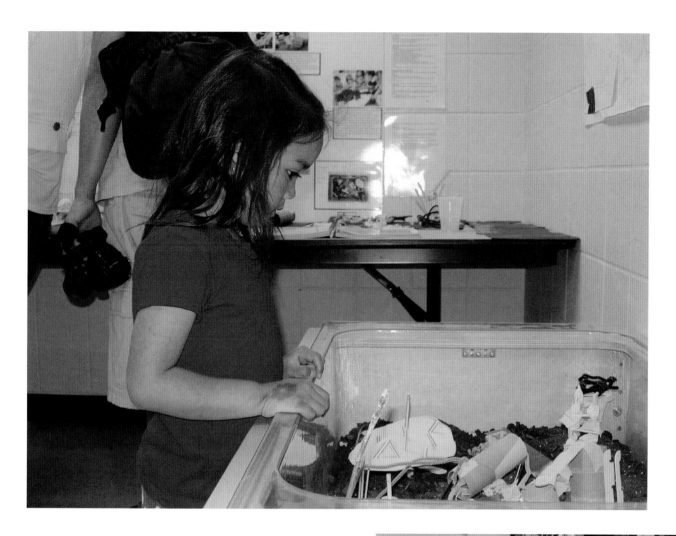

Finally, democratically, children decided that the spot next to the tree house would be the best place for the pond.

The landscape and design students' investigation culminated in a critique by professional landscape designers. Then, their work was displayed with the children's work in a center-wide exhibit held in the South Dakota Art Museum.

The planning and foundation for the playground was a positive experience, but extraordinary was the new experience of a community formed and sustained through the students' and children's active investigations. The process is transforming the Fishback Center into a learning community for adults as well as children.

A Sense of Place Impressions of the Third Street Promenade

Mary Hartzell and Joanne Mandakas

Our dialogue with the schools of the Municipality of Reggio Emilia has had a profound impact on deepening our work with children, teachers, and parents at First Presbyterian Nursery School in Santa Monica, California. We continue to benefit greatly from our ongoing consultancy with Amelia Gambetti, who challenges us to think about the why of our choices and actions. She provokes us to look more closely at our image of the child and our identity within the context of our own community.

Our school is located right in the heart of the city, where there are many rich provocations for investigation. In order to bring more focus to our work with the children, at our organizational meeting for the 2004–2005 school year we adopted an all-school declaration of intent, "A Sense of

Place: Exploring and Investigating the Life of Our School in the City of Santa Monica." This intention supported many short- and long-term explorations.

"Dogs like to walk around, look at things, bark at people."

The Third Street Promenade, which is one block away from our school, is a busy, popular walk-street filled with shops, restaurants, and theaters. In small groups, the teachers and children took many walks with specific intentions in mind. To explore their questions and theories, the children interviewed visitors and shopkeepers on the Promenade, made drawings, paintings, maps and three-dimensional representations. Also, using the language of photography, each child took a series of his own photographic impressions of the Promenade. This investigation was a strong component of the year's curriculum and maintained a high level of interest for the children until the last days of the school year.

These pages illustrate some of the many impressions and revelations of the four- and five-year-old children as they explored the Third Street Promenade.

"Some dogs are lost on the Promenade. They walk alone with no owner."

"People take walks with their dogs on the Promenade. They go there to buy things. People can buy something for the dog."

"Dogs drink and eat and maybe run in shops. It's not okay for them to do that!"

"The dogs wait for their owners when they go inside the stores, and they get tired and they sleep. Sometimes they go in the stores, but sometimes, if they have a leash, they tie them to something and they wait."

"Babies like to go to the Promenade...

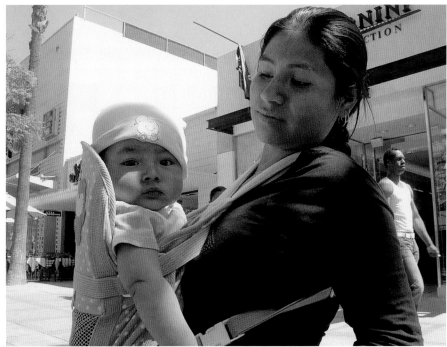

"Babies don't like to walk in the Promenade.
They like to be carried or they go in strollers."

so they don't have to stay in their backyard."

"Babies are often at coffee shops. They are getting a gallon of milk and a little treat for their moms."

"Babies play and chase birds around the Promenade. They throw crackers out to the birds. They like ice cream down the way at the ice cream store. They explore the dinosaurs squirting water and made out of leaves."

Our Environment, Ourselves

Lynne Brill and Kim Lee Ripley

*"Teachers, parents, and children working and playing together have created
a very particular space: a space which reflects their personal lives, the history
and culture of the school, and the immediate culture and geography of their lives."*[4]

LELLA GANDINI

Reggio Emilia is a place, always investigating itself.
The Hampshire College Children Center is also a
place investigating itself, with inspiration from
Reggio Emilia. Our friends and colleagues in Italy
have helped us to understand that each school has
its own history and personality, its own soul and
identity. The relationship of children with what
is around them becomes part of their identity and
culture.

Who you are is, in part, defined as where you are,
and for a very young child, it is the beginning of
how the child makes sense of her or his world.
As teachers/researchers, this daily call to define
ourselves has led us outdoors to the earth, trees,
fields, and bright blue sky that are so much of the
palette we see beyond our windows in western
Massachusetts.

Living in our environment—so full of the delights and surprises of the natural world—is an important part of our identity and culture, and is a mainstay for the children in developing a sense of self and a sense of place.

Konrad Lorenz said, "I cannot imagine how a child, who has the opportunity to come and experience the harmony of nature, cannot know that to listen to the world is a significant privilege."[5]

Our school sits on a grassy knoll (once a cornfield) on the Hampshire College campus. In one direction is a view of the undulating mountains of the Holyoke Range—verdant in summer, ablaze in color in the fall, snow covered in the winter. An apple orchard is across the street.

The college's farm rewards us with visits to the goats (their babies born each spring), llamas, pigs, chickens, and the donkey Francesca, and provides an opportunity for the children to do "chores." Some of the sheep from the college's farm center often graze in a pasture next to our school. The woods of the campus provide a wonderful landscape for walks, discoveries, and the harvesting of natural materials.

Reggio has inspired us to open our eyes to ourselves—to the "geography of our lives." The invitation to learn, research, and co-construct has led us down many muddy paths, into giant piles of leaves, and forward, to taste and treasure the crisp freshness of snow, and wonder about its magic.

Making Infants Visible

J. Ronald Lally

In the spring of 2003, the Program for Infant Toddler Care (PITC) in California brought one hundred of their professionals to Reggio Emilia for a week of conversation and discussion about the philosophy and operation of Reggio Emilia's infant/toddler programs. Of the many ideas the PITC community came away with, one was the concept of "planned visibility"— programs actively working to make the efforts of infants and their teachers visible to the larger community. We found that because of these efforts most citizens of the municipality of Reggio Emilia have come to have respect for these important members of their community, seeing infants as motivated learners and their teachers as supportive and respectful nurturers.

Annual County Fair

On returning from Reggio, our first PITC graduate conference explored many of the insights and practices our colleagues in Reggio shared with us, and how they might be blended into our uniquely California culture. Two of our graduates, Mary Anne Kreska and Annie Toors, shared their work on making visible, to the citizens of the rural county in northern California where they lived, the importance of the infancy period. To this purpose they set up, at the most highly attended event in the county—the annual County Fair—a booth that honored infancy.

Downtown Nevada City, California

Since 2003, the popularity of this installation has grown. Each year, more and more people come to see and appreciate the counties' smallest citizens in action. This visibility has led to greater community involvement in the development of quality infant/toddler child care and stronger collaborations with individuals who came to better understand the importance of infancy after seeing infants at the fair.

Photos displayed on these pages show just a few examples of how concepts first generated in Reggio Emilia touch the lives of Californians.

Creating New Visions

Dianna Smith

I've often been asked why I continue to return to Reggio Emilia year after year. This question reflects a belief that the municipal infant/toddler centers and preschools are similar in some way to other programs that offer a methodology or a curriculum that can be readily borrowed. Nothing could be further from the truth.

The programs in Reggio Emilia are based on values and beliefs that are clearly visible. Their schools are constantly evolving in ways that reflect their history, culture, and changing social values. This offers insight into why the schools provide inspiration and growth to many of us, year after year.

Visiting the municipal schools in Reggio Emilia has been a personal and professional journey, allowing me to reflect on children, teaching, colleagues, culture, environments, community, and politics over time. It has engaged me in a study of our own context here at the Campus Children's Center at the University of Vermont, full of potential and possibilities. This journey has provided new lenses for observing our youngest children well into toddlerhood and beyond. This journey has supported observation, inquiry, and collaboration to create new ways of thinking about environment, the children's process of socialization, the children's interest in authentic experiences, and their development as a school community. It has provided insight into our children's competencies, once framed and limited in our own eyes through the lens of others. It has been a study of our own children and our own values.

I have come to recognize the teacher as the essential, fundamental researcher of the children, whose knowledge, passion, and openness to the unknown allows a classroom culture to develop and flourish, revealing the children's hidden desires for meaningful relationships and genuine inquiry. Our school's journey has provided a means for our staff and faculty to work together in harmony and conflict, sharing the passion and the dream for a school worthy of the children who inhabit its structure.

I have come to realize that there will be no lasting change without widening our vision outside of school to the social and political context that provides the framework for our programs to flourish. The schools of Reggio Emilia have provided a message of hope, entwined with the clear challenge to rise above our present norms and create a new destination for our children, for our schools, for our profession.

Our colleagues in Italy have created a political voice for young children that we have yet to develop in our nation. They speak of children as "human capital" and as citizens of the present, not citizens of the future. They understand that children are producers of culture, not just consumers of culture. The educators in Reggio Emilia inspire us to elevate our public discourse to demand quality educational settings that reflect children's rights as competent, participatory citizens.

Toddlers
exploring and
taking ownership
of the University of
Vermont campus

Stories of Movement, Media, Language, and Laughter

Toddlerhood is a time of possibilities, a time when the environment abounds with experiences that are novel and unexplored. The children use these experiences to shape and reshape the meaning of their world. Toddlers possess the ability to dance with ideas; they look past the conventional and dare to experiment with the unknown. As teachers who have had the joy of building relationships with these children since infancy, we have the unique opportunity to witness and share this delightful process of inquiry and discovery on a daily basis.

We observe and interpret the children's understandings through their body language, gestures, and rapidly growing vocabulary. They seek out ways of connecting with their peers as they intersect their explorations of space, materials, movement, and language. Their stories quickly become collective knowledge in powerful, and often humorous, ways as they are repeated over and over in visual and oral language. The children's distinct ways of communicating and the stories they share become the genre of the classroom as they create a community of learners. We witness and participate in their ordinary, yet extraordinary processes of searching for meaning. As we research the "dailiness" of the exchange of ideas generated by the children, we seek to uncover the depth of their thinking and offer a classroom rich in possibilities.

Connecting and belonging…

The children are gathered around the table where everyone has a piece of clay on a spinning wheel, except Ari. His sister, Naomi, is visiting this morning, partly in celebration of his birthday. She works intently at Ari's place as he looks on.

Several minutes later there is a loud screeching sound in the kitchen area, which is surrounded by a mirror. Looking toward the mirror, we see Ari with his mouth wide open and an excited look in his eyes. He slaps the mirror and screeches again!

This is an undeniable signal. Christopher leaps from his chair and rushes to the mirror. Clio and Parker follow, joining in loud vocalizations, dancing, hand slapping, and giggling at the mirror. A toddler band is in full swing!

The children remind us that connecting and belonging are the important aspects of living. Finding common ground and common understanding are goals that we all seek. Toddlerhood motion, vocalizations, word repetitions, and much laughter offer common signals to understand one another. In an instant, Ari reveals his social awareness, his desire to connect with friends, and a very effective means to accomplish his goals!

Children as Citizens

Ellen Hall

As a result of our collaboration with the educators from the schools of Reggio Emilia and others around the world who are influenced by the Reggio schools, many aspects of our life at Boulder Journey School have evolved, including our recognition of children as citizens of the present—with inherent and irrefutable rights, including the right to participate in communities that afford them visibility and voice. Our commitment to honoring the rights of all children has resulted in the composition of a charter on the rights of children by the children of our school.

We note here an excerpt of this charter, taken from the very long list generated by the children. The rich variety in the list speaks to the power and depth of children's voices.

Children have a right to plant flowers and plants with other people.

Children have a right to grow taller.

Children have a right to run or walk, to choose which one, if it's safe.

Children have a right to have friends.

Children have a right to pretend that there's a beach anywhere.

Children have a right to pretend everything.

Children have a right to read books when they are crying (so they don't have to talk about it right away).

Children have a right to guess how things work.

Children have a right to eat grapes whichever way they choose, like peeling them first, if they want.

Children have a right to pretend being dead and think about what it means to be dead.

Children have a right to clean, fresh food to eat and if the food is dirty, they can say, "NO!"

Children have a right to know what time it is, and how many minutes they have to wait for something (their turn), and the time it will be when it's finally their turn.

Children have a right to tell parents and teachers to help them if they have a big problem.

Children have a right to solve their own problems whenever they can.

The Power of Children's Voices

Do We See Conflict as Something Only to Be Avoided?

John Nimmo

In early childhood education as I have experienced it, there is a great desire for children to be able to "get along with each other." Helping children learn to cooperate, share, and take turns is viewed by parents, as well as by teachers, as one of the most important goals and benefits of group settings. Indeed, I would agree with these goals and purposes. But one problem arises: too much stress on niceness can lead to avoidance of any conflict. Conflict refers here not to abiding anger, antipathy, violence, and hatred, but rather differing of perspectives and the possibility of co-constructing a shared understanding.

Often, when teachers engage in problem-solving and conflict resolution with children, they support the individuals in expressing their ideas and feelings ("I'm mad." "I wanted that.") but then do not proceed to help children really negotiate. This behavior, I suspect, reflects teachers' concern that they will squash one child at the expense of another if they favor a negotiation process where, yes, some individual ideas will get lost or changed, to emerge as new ideas that reflect collaboration.

The work in Reggio Emilia asks us to view intellectual conflict as a social event—even an enjoyable process. Paola Strozzi, one of Reggio's teachers, commented that young children spend a great deal of time discussing how a game will proceed, with their interest not subsiding until they have decided: "I am convinced that there is some kind of pleasure in trying to agree about how to do things." The question that arises for the teacher is whether the children are allowed sufficient freedom and opportunity to negotiate—even to argue—within the structure of the curriculum. Conflict within the envelope of a caring community is a source of growth.

Gentle Ripples of Inspiration and Change

David Fernie

The Image. My image is one of ripples in a pond, extending outward into bigger concentric circles, gently meeting other such circles. Let me explain the meaning. When I went to Reggio Emilia in 1992, I was impressed with many elements in the approach and listened closely to ideas simpatico with my own but provocatively new, deep, and interconnected. These elements and ideas are perhaps the tossed pebbles that begin the ripples for many of us. But my image is also one of change and social construction over time—the idea that many educators have been inspired by one or more aspects of the approach to closely examine their practice and to create widening concentric circles of colleagues committed to advocacy for children and families, and to our own potentials and professional growth as educators.

In the first several years after my first visit to Reggio, these dynamic and fluid circles of involvement encompassed colleagues and teachers at Ohio State, a growing professional development network of study groups in Ohio, and a group of higher education colleagues in RITE (Reggio-Inspired Teacher Education).

More recently, after taking on a new role at Wheelock College, I encountered other ongoing and exciting work—that of educators committed to exploring the pedagogy of listening and the tool of documentation with adult learners and

with children. These ripples, made by circles of Massachusetts educators involved in the Making Learning Visible Project and/or the Democracy Inquiry Group, are now beginning to flow into the activities of an ongoing circle of Vermont educators who are working in that state.

I am confident that many of us have encountered, initiated, or participated in these intersecting ripples—people in networks of intentions, explorations, and actions inspired by our experiences in Reggio Emilia and now by our own work. For me, this image is yet another meaning of the profound Reggio principle of "education based on relationships." It is truly amazing to me that, in only three decades, this one small city in Italy, its children, families, and educational leaders, has inspired countless and growing numbers of educators around the world to make connections with one another, to create feelings of "community," and to revisit and renew their commitments to young children and their families.

My Story

At the Reconceptualizing Early Childhood Education Conference in Rotorua, New Zealand, halfway around the world for me, I met and talked with a small group of local teachers one evening. Our conversation did not turn to Reggio Emilia at all that evening, but the next day, I received from a member of the group Reprovocations the gift of post cards, shown here.

I was touched, and then realized in an instant that we had, in common, drawn inspiration from the Reggio Emilia approach. The cards captured drawings made by their children in the course of a long-term curriculum project about the Kereru, a native bird of deep cultural significance in New Zealand. A sheet of text interpreted and gave context to the drawings, provided a web address for their circle (www. Reggio Emilia.org.nz), and included the following poem in Maori and English:

Whakatauki

For those who partake of the miro,
(an indigenous tree),

The forest belongs to them

For those who partake of education,

The world is their domain

Deep thanks to our colleagues from Reggio Emilia (and from around the world) for their inspiration and friendship—and for the ripples that have spread so far.

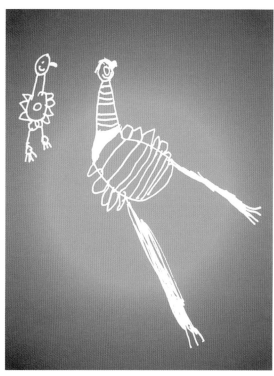

"We are working in difficult times,
   ever changing and shifting...
   beyond our ability to predict,
   for the future has become difficult to govern.

   I believe that the challenge facing children today is...
   to think how to interconnect—
   this is the watchword for the present and the future—
   a word that we need to understand deeply and in all its forms.
   We need to do so keeping in mind that we live in a world made
   not of separate islands but of networks...
   in this metaphor is contained both the construction
   of children's thought and our own thought construction...
   which belongs to a wide archipelago
   where interference, interaction, and interdependence
   are constantly present even when we do not see them."

LORIS MALAGUZZI

REchild, Reggio Children Newsletter
November, 2006, p.1

Notes

Preface

1.   page 16   C. Edwards, L. Gandini, and G. Forman (eds.), *The Hundred Languages of Children: The Reggio Emilia Approach—Advanced Reflections*, 2nd ed. (Westport, CT: Ablex, 1998), p. 10.

2.   page 19   Rebecca S. New and Moncrieff Cochran (eds.), *Early Childhood Education: An International Encyclopedia* (Westport, CT: Greenwood Publishing Group, 2006).

Introductions

1.   page 20   Carlina Rinaldi, *In Dialogue with Reggio Emilia: Listening, Researching and Learnng*, London and New York, Routledge, 2006, p. 197.

2.   page 27   Earlier versions of this introduction appeared in L. Gandini, "Fundamentals of the Reggio Emilia Approach to Early Childhood Education," *Young Children* NAEYC: Washington, DC 49, no. 1 (1993), 4–8, and L. Gandini, "The Story and Foundations of the Reggio Emilia Approach," in V. R. Fu, A. J. Stremmel, and L. T. Hill (eds.), *Teaching and Learning: Collaborative Exploration of the Reggio Emilia Approach* (Upper Saddle River, NJ: Merrill/Prentice Hall, 1997).

3.   page 28   Jerome Bruner interview, *La Repubblica*, an Italian national daily newspaper. January 14, 1996.

Section One

1.   page 32   Loris Malaguzzi, Historical Exhibit of Early Childhood Education in Reggio Emilia, 2005. This exhibit is permanently installed in the newly created Loris Malaguzzi International Center. The center is located in a recently restored historic industrial building.

2.   page 35   Howard Gardner, *The Disciplined Mind: Beyond Facts and Standardized Tests*, New York: Penguin, 2000. Chapter 5.

3.   page 41   Loris Malaguzzi, "No way the hundred is there." Translated by Lella Gandini, in *The Hundred Languages of Children*, pp. 2–3.

4.   page 47   Loris Malaguzzi, *Young Children*, NAEYC: Washington, DC. 1993. p. 10.

5.   page 48   Project Zero & Reggio Children, *Making Learning Visible: Children as Individual and Group Learners*, Reggio Children, Reggio Emilia, Italy, 2001.

Section Two

1.   page 53   Loris Malaguzzi, "History, Ideas, and Basic Philosophy: An Interview with Lella Gandini," in *The Hundred Languages of Children*, pp. 86–87.

2.   page 53   Carlina Rinaldi, *Innovations in Early Education: The International Reggio Exchange* 3, no. 4 (1996).

3.   page 58   Sue Bredekamp, "Developmentally appropriate practice in early childhood programs serving children from birth through age 8." Washington, DC: National Association for the Education of Young Children, 1987.

4.   page 62   See also "REMIDA: The Creative Recycling Center in Reggio Emilia," *Innovations in Early Childhood Education: The International Reggio Emilia Exchange,* 12, no. 3 (summer 2005).

5.   page 66   *Lesley Institutes*

1992 Environment as Teacher in the Schools of Reggio Emilia, Kindergarten Conference

1993 A Guided Journey into the Schools of Reggio

1994 Two Cultures Meeting: Adapting Practices From Reggio Emilia, Italy

1995 An Introduction to the Reggio Emilia Philosophy with some United States Adaptations

1996 Reflections on the Reggio Emilia Approach and the Basic Principles

1997 Reflection on the Reggio Emilia Approach: Philosophy and Practice

1998 The Experience of Infant/Toddler in Italy: Reggio Emilia and Pistoia

1999 Inspirations from Reggio Emilia: The Power and Pleasure of Materials

2000 Knowing Children. The Process of Observing, Documenting and Interpreting

2001 Choices We Make: Changing Perceptions of What it Means to Teach Infants and Toddlers

2002 Making Learning Visible

2003 Teachers Looking within Themselves: Professional Growth through Communication and Collaboration

2004 Building Connections: A Contextual Curriculum

2005 Approaching the Reggio Emilia Philosophy: Stories of Learning

2006 Welcoming Families, Building Community and Revisiting our Pedagogy with Infants and Toddlers

2007 Evolving Experiences within the Atelier

6.   page 79   Loris Malaguzzi, "History, Ideas, and Basic Philosophy: An Interview with Lella Gandini." In *The Hundred Languages of Children,* p. 50.

Section Three

1.   page 89   Loris Malaguzzi, "History, Ideas, and Basic Philosphy: An Interview with Lella Gandini." In *The Hundred Languages of Children*, pp. 69–70.

2.   page 89   Carlina Rinaldi, *In Dialogue with Reggio Emilia: Listening, Researching and Learning*, (NY: Routledge, 2006), p. 130.

3.   page 93   *Noi I bimbi e lui Gulliver* (We Children and He Gulliver), trans. by Lella Gandini. Published by the municipality of Reggio Emilia, 1984, pp. 28–29.

4.   page 114   Malaguzzi, L. "When we got the news" In *Brick by Brick: The History of the XXV Aprile People's Nursery School of Villa Cella*. Edited by Renzo Barazzoni. Published by Reggio Children, 2000. pp. 14–15.

5.   page 114   Terry Tempest Williams, *The Open Space of Democracy* (Great Barrington, MA: The Orion Society, 2004). p. 87

Section Four

1.   page 125   Loris Malaguzzi, "History, Ideas, and Basic Philosophy: An Interview with Lella Gandini." In *The Hundred Languages of Children*, pp. 74–75.

2.   page 136   Loris Malaguzzi, "No way the hundred is there." In *The Hundred Languages of Children*.

3.   page 136   H. Gardner, *Frames of Mind: The Theory of Multiple Intelligences* (New York: Basic Books, 1985).

4.   page 136   S. Abramson, "One, Two...a Hundred Languages: Semiotic Competence and the Reggio Emilia Approach," *Innovations in Early Childhood Education: The International Reggio Emilia Exchange* 11, no. 4, (2004), pp. 6–16.

5.   page 136   M. Danesi, *Semiotics in Language Education* (New York: Mouton de Gruyer, 2000), p. 35.

6.   page 137   S. Abramson, "Communicative Literacy,". *Co-Inquiry Journal* 1, no. 2 (2006). http:/www.coinquiry.org/

7.   page 138   Loris Malaguzzi, "History, Ideas, and Basic Philosophy: An Interview with Lella Gandini." In *The Hundred Languages of Children*, p. 74.

8.   page 141   Vea Vecchi, presentation at Winter Institute in Reggio Emilia, February 2006.

Section Five

1.   page 147   Loris Malaguzzi, "History, Ideas, and Basic Philosophy: An Interview with Lella Gandini." In *The Hundred Languages of Children*, pp. 62–63, 68.

2.   page 158   This is a reflection of the *recasting* journey of the Lugano-Reggio Teaching Research Collaborative, or the Travelers: J. Atiles, C. Bersani, T. Cacase-Beshears, P. Cruickshank-Schott, K. DeBord, G. Distler, S. Ferguson, C. D. Fernie, C. Fox, B. Gantz, A. Golden, J. Goldhaber, M. Gravett, P. Harrelsonn, L. Hill, D. Jarjoura, R. Kantor, L. Landrum, D. Lickey, K. Lyon, C. Maderni, S. Murphy, P. Oken-Wright, S. Palsha, A. Shafer, K. Singh, D. Smith, K. Snyder, S. Steffens, A. Stremmel, D. Tegano, D. Wallace, K. Wells, P. Whisnant, R. Wilkerson, and many more.

3.   page 164   See Carlina Rinaldi, *In Dialogue with Reggio Emilia*, p. 54, for the reference to Ariadne and the author's use of this myth to describe the role of the teachers.

4.   page 170   Senge, P., Cambron-McCabe, N., Lucas, T., Smith, B., Dulton, J., & Kleiner, A. (2000). *Schools that learn*. New York: Century. Pp. 52–53.

5.   page 170   F. Capra, *The Web of Life*. (New York: Anchor Books, 1996).

Section Six

1.   page 175   John Nimmo, "The Child in Community: Constraints from Early Childhood Lore." In *The Hundred Languages of Children*, pp. 300–301.

2.   page 184   The design principles presented here are drawn from two sections ("Keywords" and "Design Tools") in Giulio Ceppi and Michele Zini (eds.), *Children, Spaces, Relations: Metaproject for an Environment for Young Children.* Milan: Reggio Children (Reggio Emilia) and Domus Academy Research Center, 1998.

3.   page 186   Carlina Rinaldi, *In Dialogue with Reggio Emilia*, p. 88.

4.   page 196   Lella Gandini, "Not Just Anywhere: Making Child Care Centers into Particular Places," *Beginnings*, Summer 1984. Reprinted in *Childcare Information Exchange*, March 1991, and in 1994, 96, 48-51.

5.   page 197   Konrad Lorenz, *Autobiography Nobel Lectures*, Ed. Wilhelm Odelberg. Nobel Foundation, Stockholm, 1974.

Contributors

SHAREEN ABRAMSON, Fansler Chair for Leadership in Early Childhood Education at California State University, Fresno, is director of the Joyce M. Huggins Early Education Center, Fansler Institute for ECE, and the developer of the *Co-Inquiry Journal*.

BARBARA ACTON is executive director of The Childhood League Center in Columbus, Ohio, and former director of the Program for Young Children (PYC) at Columbus School for Girls.

JENNIFER AZZARITI, an educational consultant, was the first *atelierista* in the United States at the Model Early Learning Center in Washington, DC. She works with studio teachers in various progressive schools for young children.

PAULINE M. BAKER is a studio teacher and collaborating teacher in Tucson Unified School District's early learning programs. A consultant to Head Start and other programs in Arizona, she is cofounder of the Tucson Children's Project, an action/advocacy initiative inspired by Reggio.

CAROL BERSANI, professor at Kent State University in Kent, Ohio, collaborates with Becky Fraizer, studio teacher and instructor, and Carolyn Galizio, preschool teacher, both of whom teach at the State University Child Development Center, also in Kent.

SUE BREDEKAMP is director of research at the Council for Professional Recognition, Washington, DC, and was director of professional development at National Association for the Education of Young Children (NAEYC). Author of many publications in the field, she launched "developmentally appropriate practice."

LYNNE BRILL is the director of the Hampshire College Children's Center in Amherst, Massachusetts; she is administrator and college instructor. Kim Lee Ripley is a consultant and an infant/toddler teacher at the Hampshire College Children's Center.

JEROME BRUNER, psychologist, university professor, and scholar, is author of many books, articles, and initiatives in cognitive psychology and education. Professor Bruner is also friend to the Reggio Emilia preschools, their children, their teachers, and their educational leaders.

CAROL BRUNSON DAY is president of the National Black Child Development Institute, Inc. in Washington, DC.

SANDY BURWELL is an *atelierista*, and Audrey Favorito is a parent at the MacDonald Montessori School in St. Paul, Minnesota.

LOUISE BOYD CADWELL is an author, *atelierista*, and pedagogical coordinator at the St. Louis Reggio Collaborative in St. Louis, Missouri. She was an intern for one year in Reggio, working with the *atelieristi* of La Villetta and Diana School.

MARGIE CARTER, author and consultant, founded Harvest Resources in Seattle, Washington. Deb Curtis is an author and teacher at the Burlington Little School in Seattle, Washington. They have coauthored seven books together and travel widely to consult and present.

SIMONETTA CITTADINI-MEDINA is director of L'Atelier Preschool, in Miami, Florida, where Isabel Coles, Claudia Chaustre, and Ana Pineda are teachers.

MARGIE COOPER, president of Inspired Practices in Early Education, Inc., in Atlanta, Georgia, is also an executive board Member of the North American Reggio Emilia Alliance (NAREA).

CAROLYN POPE EDWARDS is the Willa Cather Professor of Psychology and Child, Youth, and Family Studies at the University of Nebraska in Lincoln. She has authored and edited many articles and books about the Reggio Emilia approach.

SUSAN ETHEREDGE is an associate professor of education and child study at Smith College, in Northampton, Massachusetts; her research focuses on inquiry-based teaching and learning. Martha Lees is the director of the Smith College Center for Early Childhood Education at Fort Hill.

DAVID FERNIE, a professor of education at Wheelock College in Boston, Massachusetts, researches the ethnographic study of early childhood settings, children's play, and teachers' professional development.

ANGELA FERRARIO is the U.S. liaison for study groups to Reggio Emilia and one of the founding board members of the North American Reggio Emilia Alliance (NAREA).

GEORGE FORMAN is professor emeritus in the School of Education, University of Massachusetts, Amherst; he is president of Videatives, Inc., and author of articles, books, and videos on the Reggio Emilia approach and constructivism.

SUSAN FRASER taught early childhood education in a preschool and also at Douglas College in British Columbia. Her visit to Reggio inspired profound changes in her approach to the education of young children and ECE students.

VICTORIA R. FU is an author, professor, and director of the Center for Learning and Research at Virginia Tech University in Blacksburg, Virginia.

BRENDA FYFE, author, researcher, and professor, is currently serving as dean of the School Education at Webster University in St. Louis, Missouri.

LELLA GANDINI, U.S. liaison for the dissemination of the Reggio Emilia approach, is a consultant and author of articles and books about Italian and North American early childhood education.

JEANNE GOLDHABER, researcher and author, is an associate professor of education at the University of Vermont in Burlington, Vermont.

KAREN HAIGH is executive director of the Governor State Family Development Center in University Park, Illinois, and the former director of Chicago Commons Child Development Center.

ELLEN HALL, executive director of the Boulder Journey School in Boulder, Colorado and its Teacher Education Program, is also a board member of the Hawkins Centers of Learning and the North American Reggio Emilia Alliance (NAREA), and a cofounder of Videatives, Inc.

MARY HARTZELL is director of the First Presbyterian Preschool in Santa Monica, California, where Joanne Mandakas is *atelierista*.

LYNN HILL, an educational consultant, author, and *atelierista* from Blacksburg, Virginia, has authored and edited several books about Reggio-inspired philosophy and practices.

PAM HOUK is an art and museum educator, exhibits designer, and author. Curator of the Experiencenter, Dayton Art Institute, she managed the U.S. tour of the exhibit The Hundred Languages of Children.

JUDITH ALLEN KAMINSKY is the editor of the journal *Innovations in Early Education: The International Reggio Exchange* at Wayne State University College of Education in Detroit, Michigan.

LILIAN G. Katz, widely published scholar, is professor emerita of early childhood education, editor of *Early Childhood Research & Practice*, and codirector of the Clearinghouse on Early Education & Parenting (CEEP) at the University of Illinois Children's Research Center at Champaign.

DAVID KELLY, JR., is *pedagogista* at Aquinas College Child Development Center and Grand Rapids Child Discovery Center in Michigan; he was the former exhibit designer at the Kohl Children's Museum and *atelierista* at Chicago Commons.

MARA KRECHEVSKY is an educational researcher at Project Zero at the Harvard Graduate School of Education in Cambridge, Massachusetts. With the educators of Reggio Emilia, she conducted and published research about children learning in groups.

J. RONALD LALLY is codirector of the Center for Child & Family Studies at WestEd in San Francisco, California. A researcher and author, he has been developing programs and policies for young children and their families since 1966.

SUSAN LYON is executive director of The Innovative Teacher Project in San Francisco, California, and board member of the North American Reggio Emilia Alliance (NAREA).

BETH MacDONALD is director of the MacDonald Montessori School in St. Paul, Minnesota, and board co-chair of the North American Reggio Alliance (NAREA).

PATRICIA HUNTER MCGRATH, an artist and *atelierista* in California, conducts workshops related to the integration of social constructivist practices in early childhood and symbolic languages.

SANDRA MILLER, director of the Office of Early Learning and School Readiness, Ohio Department of Education, directed the Martha Holden Jennings early childhood grant, which supported 500 Ohio teachers in their study of Reggio Emilia.

MARY MINDESS is an author and professor at Lesley University in Cambridge, Massachusetts. Marietta M. Sbraccia is staff developer and teacher at the Early Childhood Connections. Mervat Zaghbul is director of the Al Bustan Preschool, where Tazeeya Syed is a teacher.

MARY MUMBRUE taught in the Winnetka public schools for years. Her interest in the Reggio approach was sparked with a visit to the schools of Reggio Emilia in the early 1990s, when she was director of the Winnetka Teachers' Institute.

BONNIE NEUGEBAUER is editor of *Exchange Magazine*, Redmond, Washington. Author and editor, she is also chair of the World Forum Foundation with Roger Neugebauer.

REBECCA S. NEW holds a joint position in the School of Education and the Frank Porter Graham Child Development Research Institute at the University of North Carolina, Chapel Hill. She was one of the first scholars to examine the cultural and political bases of Reggio Emilia's *servizi per l'infanzia*.

JOHN NIMMO, an associate professor of family studies and executive director of the Child Study and Development Center at the University of New Hampshire in Durham, New Hampshire, is an author and contributor to early childhood publications.

PAM OKEN-WRIGHT, author and consultant, is a kindergarten teacher at St. Catherine's School in Richmond, Virginia.

ANN PELO is an author, consultant, and mentor teacher at the Hilltop School in Seattle, Washington.

MARY BETH RADKE teaches young children at the Smith College Campus School in Northampton, Massachusetts. She was a co-teacher with Amelia Gambetti in 1992–1993 at the University of Massachusetts, Amherst, Laboratory School.

BAJI RANKIN is executive director of the New Mexico Association for the Education of Young Children (NMAEC) and spent a year in Reggio Emilia studying the Reggio approach. She also taught at the University of New Mexico in Albuquerque.

Steve Seidel is director of arts in education at Project Zero, at the Harvard Graduate School of Education in Cambridge, Massachusetts. A researcher and author, he contributed to a book with Project Zero and Reggio colleagues about children learning in groups.

Sonya Shoptaugh is a teacher, author, designer, and consultant in New York City, and was formerly head teacher at the Model Early Learning Center in Washington, DC.

Dianna Smith is a lecturer in the Department of Integrated Professional Studies and professional development coordinator for the Campus Children's Center, both at the University of Vermont in Burlington, Vermont.

Andrew Stremmel is professor and head of the Department of Human Development, Consumer & Family Sciences, South Dakota University. His research focuses on teacher inquiry. Kay Cutler is an associate professor and director of the Laboratory Preschool at South Dakota University. Her research concentrates on listening and developing questions in teaching. Laura Gloege is an instructor in the department and mentor teacher in the Laboratory Preschool at South Dakota University.

Eva Tarini has taught first grade in the Winnetka public schools since 1989. She spent the 1992–93 school year as an intern in the Pablo Neruda and Diana Schools in Reggio Emilia, and wrote about her experiences there.

Pat Tarr, associate professor and author at the University of Calgary in Calgary, Alberta, Canada, specializes in art education and early childhood education. She has twice hosted The Hundred Languages of Children exhibit in Calgary.

Cathy Weisman Topal is a teacher of visual arts at the Smith College Campus School in Northampton, Massachusetts, and a lecturer in the Department of Education and Child Study at Smith. She has published several books on the arts in early childhood education.

Patricia Weissman is a preschool teacher and editor in Boulder, Colorado. She was the first editor of *Innovations in Early Education: The International Reggio Exchange*, with Eli and Rosalyn Saltz, formerly of Merrill Palmer Institute in Detroit, Michigan, and founders of the journal.

Lynn White was a first grade and kindergarten teacher in the Winnetka public schools for twenty-two years. She has been studying the ideas of Reggio since her first visit there in 1991.

Suggested Publications and Resources

Cadwell, L. *Bringing Learning to Life: The Reggio Approach to Early Childhood Education.* New York: Teachers College Press, 2002.

———. *Bringing Reggio Emilia Home: An Innovative Approach to Early Childhood Education.* New York: Teachers College Press, 1997.

Dahlberg, G., and P. Moss. *Ethics and Politics in Early Childhood Education.* New York: Routledge, 2005.

Dahlberg, G., P. Moss, and A. Pence. *Beyond Quality in Early Childhood Education and Care: Postmodern Perspectives.* London: Falmer Press, 1999.

Edwards, C., L. Gandini, and G. Forman, eds. *The Hundred Languages of Children: The Reggio Emilia Approach-Advanced Reflections* (2nd ed.). Westport, CT: Ablex Publishing Corp, 1998.

Fleet, A., C. Patterson, and J. Robertson, eds. *Insights Behind Early Childhood Pedagogical Documentation.* Castle Hill, New South Wales, Australia: Pademelon Press, 2006.

Fraser, S. *Authentic Childhood: Experiencing Reggio Emilia in the Classroom.* Scarborough, ON: Nelson Thomas Learning, 2000.

Fu, V., A. Stremmel, L. Hill, eds. *Teaching and Learning: Collaborative Exploration of the Reggio Emilia Approach.* Upper Saddle River, NJ: Prentice Hall, Inc., 2001.

Gandini, L., L. Hill, L. Cadwell, and C. Schwall, eds. *In the Spirit of the Studio: Learning from the Atelier of Reggio Emilia.* New York, NY: Teachers College Press, 2005.

Gandini, L., and C. P. Edwards, eds. *Bambini: The Italian Approach to Infant/Toddler Care.* New York, NY: Teachers College Press, 2001.

Hendrick, J., ed. *Next Steps in Teaching the Reggio Way: Accepting the Challenge to Change-Second Edition.* Upper Saddle River, NJ: Pearson Merrill Prentice Hall, 2003.

———. *First Steps Toward Teaching the Reggio Way.* Upper Saddle River, NJ: Prentice Hall, Inc., 1997.

Hill, L., A. Stremmel, and V. Fu, *Teaching as Inquiry: Rethinking Curriculum in Early Childhood Education.* Columbus, OH: Allyn and Bacon, 2005.

Katz, L.G. and B. Cesarone, eds. *Reflections on the Reggio Emilia Approach*, Urbana, IL: ERIC/EECE, 1994.

Milliken, J. *Reflections: Reggio Emilia Principles Within Australian Contexts.* Castle Hill, NSW Australia: Pademelon Press, 2003.

Project Zero & Reggio Children, *Making Learning Visible: Children as Individual and Group Learners*, Reggio Children, Reggio Emilia, Italy, 2001.

Rinaldi, C. *In Dialogue with Reggio Emilia: Listening, Researching and Learning.* New York, NY: Routledge, 2006.

Smith, D., and J. Goldhaber, *Poking, Pinching and Pretending: Documenting Toddlers' Explorations with Clay*. St. Paul, MN: Redleaf Press, 2004.

DVD: Forman, G. and L. Gandini, eds. *The Amusement Park for Birds*, Amherst, MA: Performanetics, 2006.

For a comprehensive bibliography of resources published by Reggio Children in English, visit **www.reggiochildren.it**

For more information on NAREA (North American Reggio Emilia Alliance), visit **www.reggioalliance.org**

Resources Published by Reggio Children available from:

Learning Materials Workshop
www.learningmaterialswork.com/shop/reggio.html

The Olive Press
www.olivepressbooks.com

Photo credits by page

Cover	A painting by children from l'Atelier School
15	Melissa Rivard
17	Reggio Emilia
18	Lynn Hill
20–21	Reggio Emilia
27	Pauline Baker
29	Lella Gandini
31	Lynn Hill
33	Reggio Emilia
37	Reggio Emilia
39	Reggio Emilia
47	Kate Milne
51	Lella Gandini
54–55	Brandon Phillips
87	Lella Gandini
91	Reggio Emilia
93	Reggio Emilia
94–95	Reggio Emilia
96	Melissa Rivard
121	Lella Gandini
123	Lella Gandini
132	Governor State Family Development Center
134–135	Overfield School Troy, Ohio
136–137	Reggio Emilia REMIDA
139–141	Some of the images on these pages reprinted with permission of the Publisher. From Lella Gandini, Lynn Hill, Louise Cadwell, and Charles Schwall, *In the Spirit of the Studio: Learning from the Atelier of Reggio Emilia*, New York: Teachers College Press, © 2005 by Teachers College, Columbia University. All rights reserved.
145	Lester Little
149	Reggio Emilia
158–159	Julie Bryan
165	Jen Tarr
173	Reggio Emilia
183	Dietz Architects
200–201	Mary Anne Kreska and Annie Toors
208–209	Lynn Bustle
210	Jen Tarr
211	Northcote, Auchland, New Zealand
213	Kate Nicolaou